LEADING HEALTH

HOW YOU AND 30,000 KANSANS
HELP COMMUNITIES THRIVE

ED O'MALLEY

Bard Press
Portland   New York

TABLE OF CONTENTS

PART ONE

The Health Gap

This book is about three things:

1. Kansas is ranked 29th
in the nation, according to
America's Health Rankings.*

2. Kansas used to be 8th.
That high point was in 1991.
We have been falling steadily
ever since.

**3. With your help,
Kansas can lead the nation
in Health again.**

Let me tell you how.

*Author's Note: This book was written in 2024 and quotes the latest data available from
AmericasHealthRankings.org at that time, which was the 2023 annual rankings.

CHAPTER 1

health vs. Health

Healthy citizens are the greatest asset any country could have.
—Winston Churchill

I recently attended a fascinating day at the University of Kansas Health System's main hospital in Kansas City. Every month they invite fifteen to twenty influential Kansans to their *Experience the University of Kansas Hospital* program, an event designed to share the hospital's capabilities. It's a fabulous event.

The eight-hour program is almost entirely hands-on. I inserted a chest tube into a mannequin gunshot victim. I was at the helipad when a pretend stroke victim from rural Kansas arrived on the roof. I was bedside for the removal of a blood clot in a patient's brain. Nothing felt "pretend" about it. I was sweating as if it were the real deal.

I met two amazing women physicians dedicated to treating breast cancer. They shared their cutting-edge research and left us beaming with pride that such treatment is not only available in Kansas but also was pioneered here.

Several graphs were shared during the hospital experience. "Up and to the right" was a common theme. The number of trauma victims has been going "up and to the right" for years. The number of stroke victims has been going "up and to the right" for years. Same with the number of breast cancer patients. That's true with other cancers too. While the "up and to the right" graphs were discouraging, the overall experience was amazing. I learned about technology I didn't know existed. I met brilliant doctors who lead the world at their craft.

Most attendees left the experience impressed and confident about treatments available at the hospital. I left worried. I fear our admiration for brilliant health care professionals is distracting us from understanding why our society needs more and more of their brilliance.

I fear our enthusiasm for what we can heal is blinding us to what we can prevent.

I asked each doctor I met that day what percentage of their patients' conditions were preventable. The stroke doctor said 90%. The trauma doctor said 100%. The cancer doctors acknowledged genetics are involved, but that the "up and to the right" pattern of breast cancer diagnosis is certainly linked to environmental factors like diet and physical activity. So, the dramatic increase in cases is certainly preventable.

And here's the final kicker from that experience: An emergency room doctor introduced us to a new community initiative—*Stop the Bleed*—championed in Kansas by her team. The goal? Help save the lives of gunshot victims by making sure someone around them knows how to create a tourniquet. They want *Stop the Bleed* training to be as ubiquitous as CPR training.

I'm sad there is a need for such training, but the doctors are just doing what they can do. They are trying to help. They want to save lives.

In this book, I'm making a distinction between "lowercase h" health and "capital H" Health.

Lowercase h, health, is health care. The stuff people usually think about when someone says "health." It's blood pressure and X-rays, doctor visits and surgeries. For some it's yoga, their daily workout, and taking vitamins.

"Health" with the capital H is your ability to thrive. Lowercase health is a part of Health, but only a small part. Health is everything. It's your kids becoming successful, your grandkids enjoying happiness, friendship, and love. It's the ability to control your destiny. It is agency over your life.

health = health care, sick care

Health = your ability to thrive

I started thinking about Health versus health as I drove away from that University of Kansas Hospital experience. I started to realize that health care is usually sick care. Sure, some health care is preventative, things like annual physicals and regular visits to the dentist. But the doctors I met that day, like most in the health care sector, are skilled at healing. That means the patient was sick in the first place. If I get shot, I want a trauma doctor who can help me live. But I would rather not get shot in the first place. Likewise, I would rather not have a stroke or get cancer. The day was all about health care. That's okay. The hospital's job is health care. But "Health" is about preventing the need for that healing.

The World Health Organization (WHO) defines Health as "a state of complete physical, mental and social well-being and not merely the absence of disease or infirmity." The experience at the hospital was all about treating "disease or infirmity." I'm glad we have such amazing professionals throughout our state who can help us heal from diseases and illnesses. But what about the rest of the WHO definition? Who helps ensure Kansans have the opportunity for "a state of complete physical, mental and social well-being?" I don't think those brilliant doctors and hospital administrators I met that day think of *that* as their work, although they surely agree with the definition.

Who's Responsible
for Creating Health

Last year Major General John V. Meyer III, from Fort Riley
(located in northeastern Kansas), cast a vision at an
economic conference in Manhattan, Kansas. The attendees
heard from several speakers, including yours truly, and
held numerous breakout sessions. But it was a comment
from the Major General that captivated the crowd.

Most of his speech was the typical message you would
expect from a military official. He thanked them for their
support, encouraged help for veterans, and championed
more investment for the military base. But then his speech
took a turn. He shared that his greatest aspiration is that
there will be enough Healthy Americans to continue to field
an effective military. Right now, only 31% of recruits can
pass all of the entrance requirements needed to qualify for
the Army. It's not like the other 69% just need to spend a
little time in a doctor's office or hospital and all of a sudden
they'll qualify.

"Capital H Health" versus "lowercase h health" was on my
mind as I listened to the Major General. Sixty-nine percent
of potential military recruits don't experience enough of
a state of "physical, mental and social well-being" to help
defend our country. That's a Health problem, not just a
health problem. Who's responsible for ensuring the military
has enough recruits that are Healthy?

Where you live impacts how long you will live. Let's show this by looking at pairings of life expectancy in different Kansas ZIP Codes.

66208	Mission Hills (Johnson County)	86.7
66106	Argentine (Wyandotte County)	75.1
67207	Lakewood (Sedgwick County)	82.3
67214	21st and Grove (Sedgwick County)	71.2
66044	Rural Douglas County	83.2
66743	Rural Crawford County	79.5

These figures demonstrate a disparity of over 15 years between certain ZIP Codes. And, notably, in Mission Hills vs. Argentine, the ZIP Codes are just a few miles apart, yet the life expectancy difference is over 11 years.

This life-expectancy data has me thinking about Health versus health too. Common sense suggests that the difference isn't just due to doctors and hospitals but broader issues. What difference in life expectancy is acceptable? Maybe the pragmatist in us acknowledges that the wealthy, in virtually every society, will live longer than those with less financial resources. But is that acceptable? Is that ethical? From an economic perspective, at what point does the differential become a barrier to overall prosperity of a community, region, and state?

The 30,000

This book is written for a relatively small group of people: 30,000. Quite a specific number, right? Here's how I got to it. Back-of-the-napkin style, I added up the number of Kansans in key roles of authority in our communities. This included city council members, school board members, community-minded business owners and CEOs, chamber of commerce board members, nonprofit executives and their boards of directors, pastors and rabbis and others who guide faith communities, executives and boards of state associations, executives and boards of hospitals and community foundations, school administrators, state agency executives, legislators, county commissioners, government department heads, and others. The loose math added up to 30,000 Kansans. If you're holding this book, you are likely one of those 30,000. This book is for you.

Collectively, the 30,000 are the movers and shakers of Kansas. Some of you are conservative. Others are progressive. Some are in between. Given we are in Kansas, most of you are right of center. And given we are in Kansas, most of you value working across differences, including political differences.

The Churchill quote at the beginning of this chapter applies to a state too. Healthy Kansans are the greatest asset we could ever imagine for our state.

You might not think Health is your thing. Your focus might be economic development, expanding childcare, education, or something else. But if you are reading this, I know you care deeply about your community and our state, so please bear with me for a bit. Let me show you that whatever you consider your thing in Kansas, your thing is connected to Health.

So, who's responsible for creating Health?

As one of the 30,000, Health is your job. The next chapter will show you why.

CHAPTER 2

The 30,000 and Health

I walked away from that hospital simulation experience with a provocative interpretation: The "up and to the right" data is what happens when we—the 30,000—fail to effectively exercise leadership on Health.

Our brilliant medical professionals are the experts needed to deliver phenomenal health care. But it's the 30,000 movers and shakers of Kansas who have outsized influence on the things that create the conditions for Health.

None of this is to suggest the 30,000 are wholly responsible for the Health of all Kansans. Hard work, grit, family support, and more matter. But the 30,000 have massive collective influence on factors that result in Health, like economic and education conditions. Ultimately, individuals must take responsibility for their Health. Responsibility and freedom are two sides of the same coin.

The 30,000 have the power to ensure all individuals— no matter if they are born into poverty or riches, living in a rural or urban community—have an equal shot at seizing their opportunity to create the Healthiest and happiest life possible.

We can't guarantee equal results, but we should guarantee a fair shot.

The 30,000 are a special group of Kansans. Members of this group have key authority roles, giving them the ability to focus attention, direct budgets, and cast a vision. Simply put, when you exercise leadership, you have outsized influence. Given our broad definition, Health is already your work.

The principal or manager trying to get to the bottom of absenteeism is working on Health.

The elected official considering next year's budget is working on Health.

The nonprofit board member working to improve their organization's effectiveness is working on Health.

The business owner trying to figure out how to reduce costs while keeping employee benefits the same is working on Health.

Research shows that people in your position also have better Health outcomes. Michael Marmot, author and former President of the World Medical Association, did research in the 1970s that showed a correlation between social standing and mortality rates. The research showed frontline managers had better longevity outcomes than frontline workers. Middle managers had better outcomes than front-line managers. Senior managers had better outcomes than middle managers. Senior executives had the lowest mortality rate of all, including the fewest strokes, heart attacks, and chronic diseases. Given this research, we can conclude that the 30,000 enjoy some of the best Health and lowest mortality rates in the entire state of Kansas.

But most Kansans don't enjoy that same Health and longevity. For example:

Meet ALICE

There's a group of Kansans you should know. This group struggles with Health and has grown in size as Kansas slid from #8 to #29 in the rankings. Borrowing a term from the United Way, we'll call these Kansans ALICE. That stands for "Asset Limited, Income Constrained, Employed." These are the working poor.

Here's some ALICE Threshold data:

Thirty-nine percent of Kansas households are below the ALICE Threshold. That means they don't have enough money to cover what the United Way describes as a basic "household survival budget". That budget includes basic "housing, child care, food, transportation, health care, and technology".

And worse, 60% of all Black Kansan households are below the ALICE Threshold. And 49% of all Hispanic Kansan households are below the ALICE Threshold.

While the number of Kansans under the official poverty line has remained relatively flat, households under the ALICE Threshold have grown from 28% in 2007 to 39% in 2021.

It doesn't take an expert to make a connection between the decline of Kansas Health rankings and the rise of ALICE families.

It likely doesn't matter directly to your Health whether Kansas is 29th, 45th, or 1st in the America's Health Rankings. Your Health is likely to be okay regardless. But it's a different story for ALICE.

Are the 30,000 responsible for the situation our ALICE friends are facing? No, not wholly. But yes, partly. We create conditions that influence how and if ALICE families can thrive, flourish, and be Healthy.

Will helpful actions of the 30,000 automatically improve the Health of ALICE families? No. Individuals need to make Healthy choices. But the 30,000 can make the availability and accessibility of Healthy choices easier. Individuals need to take ownership of their life and future. But the 30,000 can make sure the playing field is level.

There is a massive gap between the Health of the 30,000 and ALICE. In this book, I'm referring to that as The Health Gap. Closing The Health Gap is the key to leading the nation in Health. We won't go from #29 to #1 by making already Healthy people Healthier.

But we need a North Star, a common rallying point that the 30,000, or at least enough of us, can focus on as we go about improving Kansas. The concept of the North Star as a guiding light has its origins in its literal role in navigation. Polaris, commonly known as the North Star, holds a nearly fixed position in the sky above the Earth's northern axis, making it a reliable celestial marker for travelers and explorers, particularly before the advent of modern navigation tools. For centuries, sailors and overland travelers relied on the North Star to find their bearings and chart their courses, especially during nights when no other landmarks were visible. Over time, its dependability made the North Star a powerful metaphor for an unwavering guide or an aspirational goal. Today, we use the term "North Star" to describe a focal point or overarching aim that helps individuals and groups maintain their direction amid complexity and uncertainty.

The 30,000 have ample power to determine the direction of our communities and state. But how do they know if that direction is going up or down? What tells them that Kansas or communities in Kansas are winning or losing, getting better or getting worse? Sports teams look at the scoreboard or their win/loss record. The Chiefs look to see if another Super Bowl trophy has been added to their trophy case. Companies have a profit and loss statement. But what about us?

After twenty-five years in Kansas civic life, I crave—and know we need—a unifying metric that orients and rallies us—the 30,000 Kansans serving in key roles in our communities and state. We need a North Star that includes everything important. We need a massive proxy to help us know whether Kansas is going in the right direction or not. The right measure aligns our thinking and creates focus. Pick the right measurement and watch the magic happen. After all, what gets measured gets done.

America's Health Ranking can serve as the North Star for the 30,000. It offers a clear, stable reference point to align our efforts and prioritize actions that advance community well-being.

Let me tell you more about this North Star.

CHAPTER 3

Health as a North Star

America's Health Rankings are produced by the United Health Foundation, a nonprofit arm of United Health, the nation's largest insurance company. The fact that the rankings emerge from a health insurance company gives them more credence with me. I believe in market forces and I learned from Heather McLeod Grant and Leslie Crutchfield's book *Forces for Good: The Six Practices of High-Impact Nonprofits* that we make more progress when we leverage economic forces. It's in an insurance company's best interest for you to stay healthy. Health care is expensive. An insurance company literally makes more money if Health (and, therefore, health) improves in an organization, company, community, or state. America's Health Rankings are a communication mechanism to help people think about the factors that influence Health, which, of course, are the same factors that lead to less of the expensive kind of health care. Remember the "up and to the right" graphs I wrote about in Chapter 1? They could also describe health insurance claims.

America's Health Rankings focuses on Health, not just health care. There are over fifty measures in the ranking, covering almost everything in civic life: economic opportunity, civic engagement, education, public services, and, yes, even health care.

The fifty plus measures cover more than the traditional health care metrics, because the people behind the rankings know that what creates or diminishes health is much broader than most people realize. The measures connect education and the economy, housing and hospitals, commerce and crime. It's a massive proxy for the collection of issues important to the 30,000 and the communities you serve. You talk and hear about these issues all the time:

mental health	education
affordable housing	climate
early literacy	race
poverty	civic engagement
homelessness	health care
public safety	substance abuse
workplace safety	economic opportunity
food insecurity	health insurance
broadband	

All those issues (and more) roll up into Health and, therefore, into America's Health Rankings. It would make an excellent North Star for the 30,000. It contains almost everything important to the communities we serve. And America's Health Rankings show how Kansas is doing compared to other states on the things that matter most.

Is it a perfect ranking system? Of course not. It's a proxy. Does it lean left or right? That's in the eye of the beholder, but to me it leans both ways. People on the left will appreciate the connection to things like public health funding and vaccinations. People on the right will appreciate that most of the measures don't revolve around government. The good news is that we don't need a perfect ranking system. We just need a proxy to be our North Star.

Health Is Everything

In my early thirties, I got to know legendary Kansas State University Coach Bill Snyder because I authored the bill renaming the highway that leads into Manhattan after him. He has become a dear friend and mentor. Early on, I noticed he often asked about the Health of my family. I eventually asked him why this was a regular thing for him to ask about. His reply was simple,

"Because Health is everything."

I didn't get it then, but I do now, with more years behind me. He was speaking to a universal truth that America's Health Rankings and the Kansas Health Foundation also know. Health *is* everything, for an individual, family, team, community, company, or state. A football team won't do well if it's not Healthy, but neither will cities like Wichita, Pittsburg, Overland Park, or Liberal. The same goes for the state of Kansas.

I bet most of the 30,000 don't realize the Kansas ranking has been declining for decades. The decline isn't a warm and fuzzy thing to highlight, so I can understand why it has been ignored or downplayed. Some might fear we can't turn the tide, that we are a mere vessel floating in a national river of Health and we don't have the ability to change things. Others might feel uncomfortable calling attention to a ranking that's getting worse, despite the hard work of advocates in the Health community working for change.

But imagine a sports team discerning whether they are better this year compared to last without noting where they finished in the league standings. Or a company not focusing on market share. Or a theater troupe not focusing on critical reviews or ticket sales. Success requires some way of measuring progress. A good ranking system does that and creates competitive pressure at the same time. And when you've been precipitously sliding, the rankings make it easier to convey that slide. Of course, that only happens if you *focus* on the rankings. We adopted that focus at the Kansas Health Foundation and will do whatever we can to help others do the same.

The states are ranked every year. One to fifty. Here's the top five as I write this:

1. New Hampshire
2. Massachusetts
3. Vermont
4. Connecticut
5. Minnesota

We are getting our butts kicked by the Northeast and Minnesota. But guess what, we are also lagging behind neighbors like Nebraska (17) and Iowa (15). We are lagging other red states like Utah (9) and North Dakota (14).

Kansas should lead the nation in Health. One of the fifty states will lead the nation in Health. Why not Kansas? Right now, we are #29. We aren't satisfied with that, right? If this was the college football playoff, we wouldn't make the cut. We would be lucky to be in the "others receiving votes" category. Twenty-nine is pretty much the definition of average.

Remember that Health is a measure of nearly everything, not just health care. Twenty-one states have their act together better than we do. Their citizens are healthier, more prosperous, more engaged, suffer fewer difficulties, and have more control and agency over their lives.

I love Kansas. When you love something, you speak the truth. Currently Kansas is pretty darn average.

But the news gets worse. We used to be a top ten state. But we haven't been in the top ten since 1991. We were #8 that year and have been falling precipitously ever since.

If we had always been a bottom ten state, we might celebrate the rise to 29th. We would take stock of what's brought us so far and what remains to be done. But the Kansas story is the reverse. We have been on a steady decline.

I'm not writing this to blame any one person, faction, or organization. The truth is we—the current 30,000 and the previous "30,000"—share in the blame.

I'm the CEO of the Kansas Health Foundation. We got our start in 1985. The slide has happened on our watch. I worked for Governor Bill Graves, served in the Kansas House of Representatives, and founded the Kansas Leadership Center. The slide happened on my watch. I'm not solely to blame. But I shoulder some of the blame.

You do too.

What about individuals who let their health "go," who don't eat well and exercise, fail to get regular checkups, etc.? Yes, they are responsible too. Of course. But we can't control them. We can only control ourselves. And the 30,000 wield an awful lot of power and influence over Health.

I believe Kansas could and should be #1. Leading the nation in Health requires a ten- to fifteen-year journey. But it would be worth it, and things would look a lot different from today. Before I tell you about that though, let me describe what Kansas at #29 looks like.

CHAPTER 4

Kansas at 29th

There is much to celebrate in Kansas, but cataloging those things isn't the point of this book. The Kansas Health Foundation is made up of optimistic people. But we are also coldly pragmatic. And when you have gone from being one of the Healthiest states to being below average, we suggest putting the rose-colored glasses on the shelf.

Leadership always starts with dissatisfaction.

People who exercise leadership look at the current reality and imagine something greater. Yes, they must also be optimists, we should "first discover our strengths" and celebrate what's working. I get that. But coaching and training thousands of people have taught me leadership always, every single time, starts with dissatisfaction.

In that spirit, let me tell you about Kansas at #29. It's not a pretty picture, but one I want to describe. I promise to end on a happier note, but leadership is about naming what needs to be named, no matter how tough it is to hear.

Of the Fifty-Three Measures in the 2023 Health Rankings, Kansas Ranked

- In the top ten in just five measures
- Between 11th and 20th in ten measures
- Between 21st and 30th in eighteen measures
- Between 31st and 40th in seventeen measures
- Between 41st and 50th in three measures

Our top ten rankings are in categories like housing, renewable energy, and volunteerism. But other than that it's like I wrote earlier: pretty much the definition of average. I've included a complete list of the fifty-three measures at the end of this book. But for now let me highlight some areas we need to improve upon.

Kansas Versus Our Neighboring States

- **It's hard to breathe in Kansas, literally.** We rank 42nd in air pollution. By comparison, Nebraska is 8th and Iowa is 27th.

- **Kansas is a dangerous state, comparatively, for work.** We rank 42nd in occupational fatalities. Don't assume it's because of our agriculture and manufacturing base. Our neighboring states, with similar economies, all rank well ahead of us.

- **Being born in Kansas is relatively risky if you are a Kansan of color.** We rank 43rd in low birth weight racial disparity. Colorado is 9th. Iowa is 17th. Oklahoma is 24th. Missouri is 35th. (Interestingly, we rank 13th overall for low birth weight births. So, it's a relatively safe place to be born if you are White. But a very dangerous place to be born if you aren't.)

- **It's not easy growing up in Kansas.** We rank 38th in percent of children with adverse childhood experiences. Nebraska is 15th. Iowa is 23rd. Colorado is 27th. Missouri is 34th. In our region, we only do better than Oklahoma (41st) and Arkansas (43rd) on this measure.

- **Do you like boiling water?** We rank 38th in drinking water violations. Iowa is 6th. Missouri is 18th. Nebraska is 39th. Colorado is 43rd. Arkansas is 47th. Oklahoma is 50th.

Data Beyond the Health Rankings That Tells the Story of Kansas Too

- **Kansas concentrates the disadvantaged population.** There are neighborhoods in Arkansas City that are ranked more disadvantaged than 99% of all census tracts in the United States. In Wichita and Topeka, almost all urban neighborhoods are more disadvantaged than 90% of the United States. In both those urban areas, there are neighborhoods that literally are the most disadvantaged in all of America, scoring a 100% on the Area Deprivation Index.

- **Kansas kids in foster care have a tough road.** Just being a kid in foster care means you've had a tough life. But the foster care system alone is struggling to substantially help these kids who need us the most. Only 64% of them will graduate from high school (compared to 88% for all Kansas kids). In Sedgwick County it's even worse as only 47% of foster care kids will graduate.

- **Older Kansas kids in foster care know homelessness.** Seventeen percent of seventeen-year-old kids in foster care have experienced homelessness in the last two years. The percentage surges to 29% for nineteen-year-olds and 42% for twenty-one-year-olds.

- **Kansan Black babies and Black moms struggle.** A five-year study showed that the Black infant mortality rate was 12.1 per one thousand live births compared to 4.6 per one thousand live births for White infants.

I'm confident the 30,000 and you aren't satisfied with these data points. And, yes, I know there are a lot of other data points that are positive. But remember leadership always starts with dissatisfaction.

Leadership Requires Tough, Multiple Interpretations

Data is just data. Interpretation is what matters. How we explain things dictates how we behave. It's tempting to interpret data in ways that make us comfortable, especially for those of us in authority.

Easy Interpretations

Here are some easy interpretations related to that data, along with a bit of commentary from me:

- **"You can't trust rankings. No ranking is perfect."** In an era of click-bait headlines about the "top cities for singles" or "worst universities for free speech", I get it. But just because we can't trust some rankings doesn't mean we can't or shouldn't trust this one.

- **"It's all national trends. Kansas is just in the flow of the national river. We have little control, and everything is 'above our pay grade,' being manipulated by forces outside our influence."** I refuse to think we lack agency.

- **"Lazy, unhealthy people are to blame."** If the playing field is level and someone is still unhealthy because they aren't eating well, working out, etc., it's all on them. Until then, it's partly on them and partly on us, the 30,000.

- **"It's because of the (insert the political faction you don't like here)."** This has become the go-to in America. The political industrial complex makes a lot of money off perpetuating the rage machine that blames—always—the other.

Notice how those interpretations remove the responsibility from us, the 30,000? Those explanations place the blame elsewhere, but never with us.

Tougher Interpretations

Those serious about exercising leadership in Kansas ask themselves and others to consider tougher interpretations, such as:

- **"We rested on our laurels."** For so long we were one of the Healthiest states in America, so we simply took it for granted. We—the 30,000—didn't notice the ground shifting under our feet, or if we did, we didn't know what to do about it, or we knew what should be done but didn't know how to convince others of it. We are the state Health equivalent to the University of Nebraska football team (sorry Huskers) and companies that failed to adapt like Kodak, Blockbuster, and BlackBerry.

- **"We are an aging state, so the slide is inevitable."** Unless we grow our population, with younger individuals and families, we'll continue to slide in the rankings.

- **"The 30,000 of today and yesterday have tried countless interventions that didn't fully hit the mark."** I've lost track of how many "game-changing" economic plans have been introduced during the last thirty years. Same goes for health plans or education plans.

- **"Agreement on root causes and solutions are hard to find."** Different factions (urban, rural, conservative, progressive, etc.) are focused on their preferred explanations and solutions. Few have invested energy in trying to create a common understanding of the situation, let alone shared goals. (Hint: Leading the nation in Health is a good shared goal.)

- **"We aren't using our authority in any constructive, collective way."** We are so busy playing the part of busy people in our communities that we fail to see how our lack of coordination is part of the problem.

On deep daunting challenges, like leading the nation in Health, there isn't one correct interpretation. The leadership challenge is to acknowledge the multitude of interpretations. Recognizing there is likely truth in many of those I mentioned above and several others I could have listed.

Leadership Helps Others See Differently.

When we fail to see and consider things fully, we get caught up in the day to day. Members of the 30,000 stay busy, but their busyness hasn't shifted the underlying reality.

It's easy to confuse activity with accomplishment. Smaller things become bigger in our mind. We miss the forest for the trees.

Failing to see all this clearly has led to our steady and persistent slide in the rankings and therefore in our overall Health. Our workforce isn't as competitive. Our students aren't as successful. Our public services aren't as powerful. Our families are more fragile. Our hearts and minds are hurting.

When the 30,000 Do Rally, It's Often to Get Us to Average, Not to Excellence

- **Great work occurred recently on a massive project in Kansas called the Behavioral Health Modernization Act.** It was important and successful, but notice the word "modernization". The point was to bring us to the norm, to the average.

- **I recently heard a key official in the City of Wichita describe a need to "modernize" the city's economic development policies.** There was lots of talk of catching up to the norms in other cities.

- **"Impact investing" is the practice of foundations investing endowments in the communities they serve rather than in global markets.** Foundations have been doing this for decades. It's just beginning here in Kansas.

I applaud these efforts, but I also know that climbing the Health rankings—or doing anything that rattles Kansas out of our seemingly "average and darn proud of it" reality—requires getting beyond "catching up."

If we are merely catching up, we will forever be in the middle of the pack. And if trends continue, soon we'll be at the back of the pack.

When I took the helm at the Kansas Health Foundation (KHF) in 2022, I created a process that would ground our organization as we embarked on a bold, new strategic framework for improving Health. We engaged numerous experts and focus groups with a clear and concise question protocol, recorded and transcribed everything, and broke everything apart into individual content points. And then the themes emerged.

Kansas Civic Challenges Today Are Collective and Adaptive

Our biggest challenges are adaptive, but we also heard they are collective. One organization (a nonprofit, a county government, a church, etc.) adapting isn't sufficient. The challenges today require multiple organizations and even systems (higher education, state government, associations, etc.) to adapt together.

More specifically, from all the KHF surveys, below are the challenges that stood out. And all of them connect directly to how we are defining Health in this book.

A lack of imagination and collaboration limit economic possibilities. Our workforce size and capabilities don't match our economic needs. Rural decline offsets thriving suburban regions, creating economic stagnation at best and decline at worst. With few exceptions, fragmented, parochial economic development limits growth.

Kansans are not engaged with climate change and the social and economic impacts it is having on the state. We seem to lack the understanding of the scope, urgency, and impact of climate change. We are not prepared for the social disruption that is on our doorstep. For example, a lack of water could devastate agriculture in western Kansas, creating havoc throughout rural and urban Kansas.

Our health care system can't keep up. There is a growing lack of access to care people need at rates they can afford. Behavioral health needs are exploding, overwhelming existing providers. Too few new providers are coming to Kansas. Many in the political class have focused almost exclusively on the Medicaid expansion debate over the last decade, leaving other important health care issues to languish.

Rural Kansas's relentless decline persists. Young people leave in droves. The urge for self-preservation overwhelms imperatives for collaboration and change. Culture wars distract policymakers from the issues that could affect rural communities. Access to critical services, such as health care, fresh food, and even home building, is increasingly out of reach.

The Kansas population stagnates, ages, and shifts from rural to suburban. We continue to become a smaller and smaller percentage of the United States. We'll likely lose a Congressional representative soon. One hundred percent of our population growth over the last several decades has been because of immigration. Yet, statewide policies that might attract immigrants become lightning rod issues.

Kansans are worried about how we respond to these challenges. Here's the best way to sum up Kansans' thoughts:

What we know how to do doesn't match what's needed.

Kansans' predicament is collective, yet we focus on parochial needs. We have little shared sense of collective responsibility, agency, or urgency to address challenges.

Stratification across political differences is increasing. This type of politics seen in Washington, DC infiltrated the politics of our state government in Topeka a decade ago. Now it's trickling down to our county governments, city governments, and school boards.

Everything is becoming more political in Kansas, as is the trend in America. Kansans are sorting themselves into two meta factions, one on the left and one on the right. Organizations that traditionally aren't directly engaged in politics are struggling to navigate this new world. For example, local chambers of commerce—traditionally beacons for consensus-building policies to support economic growth—struggle to word legislative agendas so they don't trigger anyone. All this political polarization—which is, of course, part of our national story—limits our capacity to cope with the collective and systemic challenges.

In short, Kansans have been dealt a tough hand and aren't playing it well. For those who love Kansas, this chapter has likely been hard to read. It was certainly hard to write! Let's turn our attention to aspirations and dreams and imagine what Kansas would be like if we overcome these challenges and lead the nation in Health.

CHAPTER 5

Kansas at #1

Exercising leadership requires a ruthless balancing of pragmatism and idealism. On the one hand, we need to be frank about what's possible. On the other hand, we need to describe a future worth striving for. The last chapter was about pragmatism. This chapter is about idealism. The last chapter stated plainly the concerns facing Kansas when it comes to Health. This chapter paints a picture of what things could be like if we lead the nation in Health.

If Kansas led the nation in Health, our economy would be stronger. Businesses and workers would want to be in Kansas. Employer health insurance costs would be low. Productivity would be high. The workforce would be a match for the global moment. The challenges we hear today from businesses about employee mental health issues, substance use disorders, and lack of skills would recede.

Communities would be more vibrant. Crime would be lower. Neighborhoods would be safer. Urban centers and rural downtowns would be markets of opportunity and commerce.

Families would thrive. More Kansans would control their destiny. They could live lives of consequence. Less energy would be spent coping with poverty. More energy would be spent flourishing.

Individuals would have an equal chance. The deck wouldn't be stacked against anyone. Personal skill and effort would determine whether someone gets ahead or not. Everyone would have agency. Barriers to participating in community and economic prosperity would be minimized or eliminated. Kansans—as individuals and as a whole—would simply be *Healthier*.

It's an exercise of leadership to cast a vision. It's especially important for the 30,000 to cast a vision. That vision should be informed by listening deeply to stakeholders and should reflect their hopes and dreams. But, ultimately, it takes someone with authority, credibility, and standing in a community, organization, or system to cast a vision.

I'm doing that with this book. Some of you do it too. A nonprofit's exec casts a vision to end homelessness. A Speaker of the House casts a vision to make Kansas competitive for investment and business growth. A CEO casts a vision to retain and attract talent so the company can thrive. All those aspirations come back to the topic of Health. They all roll up into the North Star. These aspirations describe a future state. Getting from here to there is the key. Momentum is created when people describe the future they desire, for themselves, but especially for their families, neighborhoods, and communities.

In some ways, our aspirations are just the flipside of our concerns. A concern might be too many nonprofits working on the same mission but with little synergy. The related aspiration might be a streamlined nonprofit sector working in sync and maximizing impact on the issues that matter most.

Another concern might be the lack of economic opportunity for those below the ALICE Threshold. The related aspiration might be an ample opportunity for economic mobility for all.

Talking about concerns creates a necessary, but frankly, somewhat negative energy. It's the necessary pragmatism coming through. Talking about aspirations—such as Kansas leading the nation in Health—is different. The energy is generative and positive. It unlocks and unleashes the idealism necessary for progress on daunting leadership challenges.

Here's What I've Learned About Kansans' Aspirations

1. **Kansans believe we can do better.** Our aspirations don't feel out of reach. Kansans know the right energy focused in the right direction with the right people gets results.
2. **Kansans believe we must be bold.** In countless ways, Kansans have conveyed to me that a lack of bold visions is a barrier to progress. We know something happens when people dream bold dreams. And Kansans know we need more of that in our organizations and communities.
3. **Kansans believe seizing aspirations is collective work.** Kansans want us all to work together. They know Kansas leadership—the 30,000—must work together.

But casting bold aspirations feels risky. Trust me. I know. Personally, things would be easier for me if KHF hadn't cast a vision for Kansas to lead the nation in Health and to climb to number one in the rankings. It would have been easier and safer to simply have a fluffy, generic vision. To improve Health for all. To make Kansas a great place for families. To make things better. Yawn.

Bold visions are risky.

The bolder the vision the less certain you can be about success. A bold vision like leading the nation in Health is also easy to assess. The rankings come out every year! It will be obvious if we are or are not successful. And we all know what happens to CEOs of organizations that are obviously unsuccessful.

The bolder the vision the more critique about what's included. Boldness attracts attention, good and bad. Mild aspirations are ignored, but that means they aren't critiqued either. But the risk is worth it. The energy unleashed from bold aspirations fuels leadership and progress. In that spirit, let's get some of that positive energy flowing as we explore what Kansas would look like if it led the nation in Health.

Aspiring for Number One

We'll make this real by comparing Kansas and New Hampshire. In the America's Health Rankings Kansas is 29th and New Hampshire is 1st. If Kansas had the ranking of New Hampshire, and we adjusted the population numbers accordingly, it would literally mean:

- **105,000 fewer Kansans would be hungry.** It's hard to be a productive member of society when you are hungry. Here's a light-hearted example: My wife gets "hangry." Maybe you can relate to this quasi-emotional/physical state created when being hungry morphs into being angry. All kidding aside, imagine how hard it would be to learn in school, succeed in the workforce, and get along with your neighbors when you are hungry. Now imagine how much better things would be in Kansas— for individuals and for all of us—if 105,000 fewer people were food insecure.

- **32,000 more Kansans would be reading at grade level by fourth grade.** That means everything gets easier for those kids in school, that leads to more success for them and their future families. It also means schools can expend fewer resources helping students catch up later. It means 32,000 more Kansans right now would be on track for becoming contributing, engaging, and productive members of our Kansas communities.

- **173,000 more Kansans would exercise regularly.**
  In addition to all the physical benefits those Kansans
  would enjoy, it's also 173,000 more Kansans who
  would experience the emotional uplift that comes with
  regular exercise. That's additional Kansans in your
  workplace, family, school, and neighborhood who are
  healthier and happier.

- **183,000 fewer Kansans would be engaging in non-
  medical drug use.** That's 183,000 more Kansans
  not needing controlled substances to cope with their
  situation. That's fewer Kansans becoming addicted,
  fewer families struggling with how to help their loved
  ones in the grip of addiction. It also means existing
  resources to help those battling substance abuse can go
  further. It means more Kansans would be able to pass
  necessary drug tests for employment.

I could go on. And to be fair, there are a few of the fifty
plus measures where we are ahead of New Hampshire.
But overall, New Hampshire is winning the Oscar, capturing
the Grammy, lifting the Vince Lombardi Trophy, and
cutting down the nets.

Your work directly connects to several of the fifty plus
measures in the ranking. Indirectly it connects to most of
them. The 30,000 and you have more power than any
other group to influence the conditions fueling the "up
and to the right" trends I wrote about earlier. You have
an outsized influence on the existence of The Health Gap

and an outsized ability to eliminate it. The Health Gap is
a collective leadership challenge for the 30,000.

It's up to the 30,000 whether Kansas leads the nation in
Health. No one else can focus the energy, resources,
and attention to climb from 29th to 1st. There are conservative and progressive ways of leading Health. There
are multiple ways forward. Before we debate strategies,
we must realize:

Health already is your work.
Leading Health is your opportunity.

Health Is a Leadership Challenge

Passionate people working for change are often their own biggest enemy.

An advocate for the homeless is so focused on her cause, that she fails to see connecting interests with other groups or factions. She sees herself as a hero, leading important work for the greater good. But a lack of understanding of how to grow the coalition of organizations on board with her vision stymies progress.

A speaker of the house knows everything in Kansas gets worse if we don't grow our population in real numbers and in our percentage compared to the United States. He's right. But a lack of clear focus on this obviously urgent issue leads him at the end of two years with no more of a coalition focused on growing Kansas than he had when he began.

A business executive, with a heart for community, wishes to use his authority to create game-changing progress on mental health reform. He knows we need a dramatic increase in the mental health of the workforce. But an inability to recognize that leading in community is different than leading in business thwarts his efforts.

In these examples, the real challenge was different than it first seemed. The advocate thought the challenge was homelessness. The real challenge was discovering connecting interests with others. The speaker of the house thought the challenge was population growth. The real challenge was using his authority to grow the coalition of organizations who share that focus. The executive thought the challenge was the mental health of the workforce. The real challenge was understanding what's required for progress in civic versus business life.

Those of us who care about Health, and by now I hope that includes you, fall into this trap too. Improving Health is a leadership challenge, not a health challenge.

Doug Easterling is one of the most passionate and smartest people I know working on The Health Gap. A professor at Wake Forest University, Doug has dedicated his career to improving Health in communities across America. He's been a friend and advisor to me for years. He summed up our approach best at a recent retreat of key KHF advisors when he said:

> You're not using a medical model to improve Health. You're also not using a public health model. Yours is a leadership model for improving Health. It's totally different than the dominant approaches.

As usual, Doug nailed it. Yes, the topic is Health. But all my experience in civic life, all my experience coaching and building capacity in others to solve daunting challenges, and all our collective experience at KHF suggest that while the topic is Health, the answer is leadership. From you. From me. From the 30,000. And, in time, from many more.

At the risk of leaning too heavily on a medical metaphor, I offer up a summary of this book. Part One described the symptoms. Part Two will give a diagnosis. And Part Three outlines the prescription.

Part Two explores the problems behind the problems. The very problems that people like you, the 30,000, need to address.

Closing The Health Gap is a leadership challenge. It's not something to just leave to medical experts and public health professionals. Those people have a part to play. But it's just a part. This isn't a one-person band or a monologue on stage. Progress requires an orchestra, a marching band, a whole cast for the play or an entire theater troupe.

Closing The Health Gap is not a health care challenge.

It's not a public health challenge.

It's not a nutrition and fitness challenge.

It's not a challenge Ozempic can solve.

Even if all the experts on health care, public health, nutrition, fitness, and wonder drugs do their part, the gap will remain. That's because The Health Gap is first and foremost a leadership challenge for the 30,000.

CHAPTER 6

It's a Leadership Challenge, Not a Health Challenge

We each spend our days solving countless challenges. The car breaks. We fix it. Someone doesn't show up for work. We cover the shift. The bills come in. We pay them.

But we also spend our days *not* solving countless other challenges. The drama between team members continues to fester. We avoid it. A married couple grows distant from one another. With each passing day the distance gets greater. We notice a growing number of people living on the street. We go on with our day. After all, we have a car to fix, a shift to cover, and bills to pay.

Some challenges need good execution. Others need good leadership. Knowing which challenges require which is the key. The Health Gap needs leadership. This is a leadership book, so I should be clear with what I mean by leadership.

Leadership Is Mobilizing Others to Make Progress on Daunting Challenges

Leadership is an activity, not a position. It's a verb, not a noun. (Not technically in that sentence above, but you get the idea!) Whether you've done it or not—whether you have exercised leadership, or not—is directly related to whether others have been mobilized and progress has been made.

Your title doesn't make you a "leader". It makes you someone with a title, with authority. Good for you. Whether you exercise leadership is a totally different question.

Leadership on The Health Gap? We'll explore why it's so hard throughout Part Two. Not only is it hard, but it's also rare. Are there a lot of wonderful, passionate people working hard, day in and day out, to improve Health? Of course. And still we've slid so far in our ranking as a state. Working hard and having passion aren't the same as exercising leadership. Here's a way to think about it:

You can't exercise leadership on Health without a lot of passion and hard work. But just being passionate about Health and working hard doesn't mean you are exercising leadership. It doesn't mean The Health Gap is any smaller. It doesn't mean progress has been made. Leadership is all about progress. Period.

Notice I'm using the word "leadership" not "leader." I love the word leadership. I hate the word leader. Why? Because too many people get called "leaders" when they haven't exercised leadership. Whether they exercise leadership or not is the fundamental question. I refuse to call someone a leader if they aren't exercising leadership.

Leadership is mobilizing others to make progress on daunting challenges.

This chapter explains, at a high level, why The Health Gap is a leadership challenge. The rest of the chapters in Part Two describe the details of how this leadership challenge—closing The Health Gap—plays out in Kansas.

At a high level, The Health Gap is a leadership challenge because of three factors. First, because it is important but rarely feels urgent. Second, because it requires adaptation for progress. And third, because progress requires a clash of values.

The Health Gap Is Important but Rarely Urgent

Like a lot of leadership challenges, making game-changing progress on Health is one of those classic "important but rarely urgent" issues. When it gets urgent is often when we need health care. Sick care.

Health the way I've been writing about it here is usually on the back burner for most people. They can start taking walks tomorrow. They can review the company's wellness policies next quarter. They can review the city or county policies for how they impact Health next year.

Leadership pro-tip: Those skilled at exercising leadership help others bring issues from the back burner to the front burner. Not all back burner issues are leadership challenges. But every leadership challenge, until the heat is high enough, will look like a back burner issue. There will always be other things you feel need more of your time and attention. Which is why:

The Health Gap Requires Adaptation

Some challenges are more vexing than others. What's needed for progress depends on the nature of the challenge. Do you need to raise or lower pressure on others? Do you need to engage more or fewer people in problem-solving? Do you just solve the challenge alone? Do you need to go fast or slow? Some people know the answers intuitively. Others learn over time. I was somewhere in between.

Serving in the state legislature at a young age was a crash course in human dynamics and problem-solving. It taught me how people make progress and, more often, what they did to screw it up. I learned progress on the toughest challenges required humility, listening, and collaboration. I saw progress happen when people came together to make it happen.

I learned leadership was about helping those people come together, not having the right answer yourself. But there was so much more I needed to learn.

I left politics to start the Kansas Leadership Center in early 2007. Not long after I met Marty Linsky and Ron Heifetz from the Kennedy School at Harvard. During our early listening, Kansans gave voice to a potential leadership framework. Marty and Ron brought it to life for us. They had pioneered thinking about progress on the toughest challenges around. They were thinkers, practitioners, and teachers. Ron was a physician turned academic. Marty came to academia via politics. They collaborated to create a framework for making progress on what they call "adaptive challenges." Their book, *Leadership on the Line*, was game-changing for me.

Closing The Health Gap is an adaptive challenge. KHF and I are trying to bring The Health Gap to the front burner. With this book I am trying to raise the pressure on the 30,000, myself included. The slide from #8 to #29 should create urgency. If the trends continue, our families, co-workers, and community members will struggle more and more in everything from their health to their education to their livelihood.

Marty and Ron, as well as my almost sixteen years at the Kansas Leadership Center, taught me progress will require adaptation. We'll need to change what we do and how we do it to get more progress. That kind of change requires leadership, from you and from me.

Progress on The Health Gap Requires a Clash of Values

Adaptive challenges like closing The Health Gap always involve a clash of values. You might jump to thinking about a clash between progressive or conservative values. That's at play, of course, but there are harder, sneakier, and, frankly, more important value clashes at play.

A family says it values Health but doesn't utilize any of the preventative services associated with its health insurance plan. A company says it values the Health of employees, but the only time Health is explicitly discussed is during the once-per-year open enrollment insurance period. A school district says it values the Health of students, but then "serves mass-produced food full of additives in the cafeterias. A state says it values the Health of its citizens, but its Health ranking has slid from #8 to #29.

It's not that the family, company, district, and state don't value Health. They do, but it's clear they value other things more. Raise your hand if you are opposed to Health. No one will raise their hand. Everyone is for Health, but if it is the seventeenth thing on your list of things you care about, your behavior might not be very different than if you didn't value it.

Leadership on adaptive challenges involves helping people negotiate competing values. What are some of the competing values related to Health in Kansas? Here are three examples.

Those exercising leadership on Health help others see these clashes and negotiate a way forward despite the conflict.

- **Individual versus collective responsibility.** The leadership challenge here is to help others understand that it takes both individual and collective actions to make progress. The question is where to draw the line between the two, not whether the line exists.

- **Important versus urgent.** An individual pushes off starting an exercise program because they are consumed with getting this project or that task done today. An organization has good intentions to start a mental health first aid program, but deadlines related to a big deal take precedent. A city wants to launch a wellness program for staff, but...you get the idea. Leadership is about helping the things that are important, but not urgent, get enough attention to promote action and eventually progress.

- **Private sector versus public sector responsibility.** Some value private sector interventions. Others believe the point of the public sector is to ensure things like Health. Those exercising leadership on Health help people find the right mix for their context, which will obviously be different if you are in the United Kingdom with its National Health Service or in the United States with our mix of private and public insurers. And, further, if you are in a red or blue state. There's not one universal correct answer. But there is a right answer for your context. Those exercising leadership on Health help their people find the right answer.

The goal when exercising leadership isn't to have what you value crush what someone else values. It's always more synergistic. It's helping people understand and appreciate what others value and helping people negotiate all those values into a way forward that works for everyone, or at least enough of everyone. That's adaptive work. It requires leadership. From you, me, and others.

Closing The Health Gap isn't just a leadership challenge, it's one of the most vexing and most important public and civic challenges in Kansas. The rest of Part Two will highlight more aspects of this leadership challenge, describing what makes progress hard and giving you new ways of thinking about The Health Gap and your role in it.

CHAPTER 7

It's a leadership challenge because

We Don't Agree on What Caused the Problem, or the Solutions

Here's a tell-tale sign you have a leadership challenge on your hands. Virtually everyone agrees there is a problem but there isn't agreement on the reason for the problem or the solutions needed. For example, I can't imagine there is anyone reading this book who likes the fact that we've slid from #8 to #29 in the rankings. We agree that's a problem. But the cause of the slide? How to turn it around? No clear agreement there. Which is why leadership is required.

Exercising leadership on a challenge like The Health Gap looks like creating alignment (or at least as much alignment as possible) on how people define the problem(s) as well as the solution(s). It will never be complete alignment. But progress requires better alignment, more consensus, more synergy with how different groups, factions, and organizations, within the 30,000 and beyond, think about the problems and solutions related to The Health Gap.

Ideally, there would be as much alignment as possible on how hospital executives, doctors, mental health professionals, insurance companies, nurses, public health officials, and others in the health care sector think about The Health Gap. And, ideally, that alignment would extend to state and local elected officials, nonprofit executives, chambers of commerce, business CEOs, education professionals, city and county administrators, and all the 30,000 we are referencing in this book.

The challenge, of course, is that we are almost hardwired to do the opposite of creating alignment. When a problem is complicated, complex, and daunting, human nature searches for the easiest explanation—for us, for our faction, for our group—for why the problem exists and how to solve it. Three things usually emerge when that happens.

First, our initial explanations (I like the word "interpretations") almost always place the blame somewhere else. The situation isn't our fault. Our preferred interpretation blames someone else or some other group. But rarely us. Progressives and conservatives blame each other for the ills in our country. Workers blame executives and vice versa for the problems in our companies. Health care people blame policymakers. Policymakers blame health care people. And on and on it goes.

Second, our initial interpretations almost always assume there is a relatively quick fix. The person fed up with polarization of politics in America is certain a viable third party is what's needed to reduce polarization. The advocate for the ALICE population is certain that expanding Medicaid solves the Health challenges of the working poor. The legislator passionate for literacy assumes getting books into every child's home is the key.

Third, our preferred explanations almost always require change, just not change for us. Primary care physicians should add a screening for this or that condition to their checklist with each patient. But our company? No, there's nothing we need to do differently. The other political party should change their thinking. But our party? No, we're good! Oh, and when our preferred explanations do require change for us, it usually is only the good kind of change. Yes, my agency will gladly accept a $500 million increase to our annual budget! Yes, I will gladly let someone else do all the work I hate doing. We are all in for those kinds of changes.

In summary, how we interpret, or understand, a situation often controls how we act to solve it. If we think the problem with education is a lack of funding, we add funds. If we think the problem with fitness is a lack of parks, we add parks. If we think the problem with health care is insurance coverage, we create ways of covering more people. The Health Gap is a leadership challenge because it requires us—lots of us—to question our interpretations, to imagine even more interpretations, and to help others do the same. We must disrupt the narrative.

A narrative is just our version of the truth. As we've already explored throughout this book, there are massive discrepancies regarding what different groups and factions feel is "true" when it comes to The Health Gap. Civic life in America today looks like a lot of people rallying around their version of "the truth," getting constant reinforcement from those whose opinions matter most to them. The following passage from Thomas Merton, a great American theologian and writer, is heady but explains perfectly what I'm getting at here:

> The basic falsehood is the lie that we are totally dedicated to truth, and that we can remain dedicated to truth in a manner that is at the same time honest and exclusive: that we have the monopoly of all truth, just as our adversary of the moment has the monopoly of all error.

> We then convince ourselves that we cannot preserve our purity of vision and our inner sincerity if we enter into dialogue with the enemy, for he will corrupt us with his error. We believe, finally, that truth cannot be preserved except by the destruction of the enemy— for, since we have identified him with error, to destroy him is to destroy error. The adversary, of course, has exactly the same thoughts about us and exactly the same basic policy by which he defends the "truth." He has identified us with dishonesty, insincerity, and untruth. He believes that, if we are destroyed, nothing will be left but truth.

And he wrote that in the 1950s! While he is using strong words like monopoly of all error, destroy him, adversary, and enemy, the dynamic he is describing is at play in so much of the leadership challenge that is The Health Gap. We must disrupt our own narrative just as much as our opponent or enemy's narratives.

Progress on deep, daunting, adaptive challenges almost always requires disrupting existing narratives.

Your own narratives and the narratives of your opponents. Let's get clearer about what this looks like regarding The Health Gap.

When the problem is technical, the "problem definition" is clear. The X-ray shows a bone is broken in a child's femur. The test results confirm a cancerous tumor in a senior citizen. Technical problems have clear solutions. Set the bone and put the leg in a cast. Remove the tumor and begin radiation and/or chemotherapy.

Everything is different with an adaptive challenge like The Health Gap. Ask ten plugged-in Kansans why we've been sliding in the rankings and you'll get ten different answers. Some will say the problem is that the state hasn't expanded Medicaid. Others will say people aren't taking personal responsibility. Some will say our economy has created a health care/sick care industrial complex that is out of control. Others will say we have too many regulations that are killing the chance for innovation related to Health.

The likely truth is it could be all those things and many more.

Adaptive challenges resist clear solutions. Do we solve
The Health Gap by increasing public health funding?
By encouraging private sector innovation in Health?
By encouraging more individual responsibility? By training
health care professionals differently? By encouraging
more people to go into health care fields? Yes. And probably
a lot more things too. Deciding what to do or what
to stop doing fosters strong and divergent opinions.
See the problem?

What Makes It Hard to Align around Common Problem and Solution Definitions

My experience tells me agreement is hard for three reasons:

- **Expectations.** People in authority, people like the 30,000,
  are expected to have answers. The mayor is supposed
  to have a plan for solving homelessness. The Speaker of
  the House is supposed to have a plan for growing the
  state's population. The CEO is supposed to have a plan
  for solving the mental health crisis facing her workforce.
  People in authority aren't often rewarded for asking big,
  open-ended questions. Which is too bad, because we
  need their help in putting the big, open-ended questions
  in front of us, so we can learn to think differently and
  work differently on the problem.

- **We don't see the lack of alignment as a big enough problem.** We spend time on what we think needs the most of our time. We just don't realize that creating alignment is where our time is needed! Therefore, we don't value it and limp along with a lack of alignment, lack of agreement, or lack of consensus. It takes time to diagnose things well, and if we don't do that, we won't get agreement on the real root causes of the problem, let alone effective potential solutions.

- **We oversimplify.** The totality of the problem is so great that we fall victim to oversimplification. We get too loyal to the part of the problem we connect with most. Here's a Health example in Kansas. I'm in favor of Medicaid expansion. Unfortunately that debate has sucked the life out of so many other necessary discussions for improving Health in Kansas in the last decade. Do we need Medicaid expansion? I think so. Is it the only thing we need to go from 29th to 1st? No. Not even close. Can we get from 29th to 1st without it? Yes. And to do so we will need a lot more people to have quality insurance coverage.

Use Your Authority to Help Your Group or Faction

Resist trying to define the whole problem. Instead, start by just defining your part of it. When the challenge is adaptive, we all have a part to play in the mess. I'm not saying you are to blame for The Health Gap in your community, our state, or your organization. But I am suggesting that you own a piece of it. This is classic wisdom. Almost every spiritual tradition has a version of "before criticizing the speck in your brother's eye, remove the plank in your own eye."

Spend more time defining the cause of the problem. An authority simply asking her group "Why are we defining the problem the way we are?" goes a long way. I've been a part of countless meetings about how to do right for the northeast Wichita community who has suffered—through no fault of their own and without transparent communication from civic authorities—from horrific groundwater contamination. For over eighteen months a group who wanted to create accountability and justice had made little progress. And then we started to inspect how we were defining the problem. We had been thinking about it from an individual lens, leading us to think about solutions for each of the potentially forty thousand individuals affected. Because of a skillful intervention from the CEO of a key local health clinic, we shifted our thinking to defining the problem and the solutions more systemically. We began to think and create solutions in the broadest terms possible. I'm leaving out a lot of detail here, but the shift in thinking moved us from being in a logjam to having major forward momentum.

Make sure people know the difference between goals and strategies. That means framing the issue as "reducing the number of uninsured" (which is the goal) rather than as "expanding Medicaid" (which is a strategy). Or "creating conditions for people to live Healthy lives" (the goal) rather than as "encouraging personal responsibility" (a strategy). Use your authority to help your people be more loyal to goals than their preferred strategy.

Benjamin Franklin famously said, "He who sets the agenda controls the outcome." That's what we are talking about here in this chapter. Too many of us fail to "set the agenda" in a way that is conducive for progress. Use your authority to create alignment on the problem definitions and the solution definitions related to Health.

Here are some examples:

A vice principal oversees reducing the skyrocketing number of student absences in her high school. At a staff meeting, the teachers and other administrators want to jump to ideas about increasing consequences for missing school. But she forces discussions about "why" there is an increase in absences, wanting to help everyone have a better, deeper diagnosis of what's causing the problem.

A state official is working to transform behavioral health services in Kansas. Stakeholders around the state want to discuss increasing Medicaid payments for services. He knows that's important, but forces discussion instead about what's happened in Kansas since we lost the world's premier behavioral health center, the Menninger Clinic, in the early 2000s. He's using his authority to help stakeholders see a deeper, more complicated, picture about why we used to be in the lead on behavioral health and now we are a laggard.

A CEO of a business is trying to reduce health insurance increases that are crippling the company budget. Her vice presidents want to focus on getting quotes from other insurance providers. The CEO instead launches a deep listening project to understand how employees feel about their Health and what they think influences it the most. That listening leads everyone to understand the problem isn't the insurance carrier but rather the lack of a culture of Health and wellness.

A Health foundation CEO uses his authority to cast a massive vision for his state. And he simultaneously publishes a book to compel state leaders to have open and active discourse about the vision. In the book, the CEO also encourages those leaders to invite others from their organizations and communities to engage in these conversations.

Your authority can help create more alignment around the causes of and possible solutions to The Health Gap—in your organization or community as well as across our state. Your authority is a resource. Use it to create alignment, not division. Use it to create integration, not separation. Use it to frame Health issues productively. Use it to help others see surprising connections to Health that disrupt their narrative. Use it to help others see their part of the mess. Do that by modeling that you understand your part of the mess. Use your authority to help others become loyal, first and foremost, to the goal of Health.

CHAPTER 8

It's a leadership challenge because
Our Existing Assumptions Fail Us

You get called a leader often. So do I. It feels good, doesn't it? But I'm not buying it and I don't think you should either. By now you know I believe leadership is an activity, not a position. Leadership is a verb, not a noun. It's something you do, not a role you play. Leadership is mobilizing others to make progress on daunting challenges. Did you do that today? Did I? The point is, you would need to watch me to know if I exercised leadership. Did I mobilize people to close, even just a little bit, The Health Gap today? This week? This month? This year? Did you?

What exercising leadership looks like depends on the challenge, and the skill and experience of the person exercising leadership. But one thing never changes. The person exercising leadership must be very conscious of their own thinking and assumptions. They must be able to think about their thinking. I know, that's meta. Here's a little example:

My son Jack played a lot of basketball growing up. I had the privilege to coach his teams. He was, and still is, a gifted player, and a smart one too. By the time he was in middle school we could talk about the mental side of the game in ways you just can't with a little kid. I always led with the same question whenever he wanted to debrief a particular play in a game. "What were you *thinking about* when that play happened?"

I promise it wasn't the overly aggressive youth sports coach yelling, "What were you thinking?!" It was subtle and nuanced. I was trying to get him to rewind the tape and think about what thoughts—specifically what assumptions—he was making that led him to do whatever he ended up doing on the court. I was trying to help him become more conscious about those assumptions. Why? Because on the basketball court, as in the boardroom, or at the company executive meeting, the assumptions we make almost always control how we behave.

If Jack assumed his teammates couldn't score inside against the other team's height, he might stop passing to them and instead take the outside shot himself.

A nonprofit executive assumes the monthly ninety-minute board meeting is the way the board prefers to meet. Despite that time never being enough for her to facilitate the deep, strategic discourse she craves and needs from the board. Her assumption keeps her from even suggesting switching to a quarterly full-day meeting instead.

A corporate CEO assumes her company is doing all it can to help support the mental health of her employees. Her assumption keeps her from considering additional support or from even inquiring about the topic with her team.

A state legislator assumes he can't influence Health. His assumption keeps him from paying attention to the Health rankings and discovering the part he can play.

What assumptions are you making? People want to believe those in authority roles—that's likely you if you are reading this book—have well thought-out assumptions and that your assumptions are clear to you and informed by evidence. But the reality is you and I are often just like that nonprofit executive, CEO, and state legislator I mentioned above.

Closing The Health Gap will require a lot more of us to become more conscious about the assumptions we are making related to Health, our role, and how to make a difference.

This is critical for two reasons. First, the more conscious we are about our assumptions—our default thinking— the better we'll be at making choices that propel progress. Second, not being more conscious can make The Health Gap wider and make working on all the issues connected to Health harder. Our assumptions can create harm if we aren't careful! I learned that from Kevin Bomhoff, one of the wisest, kindest, and most passionate Kansans I know.

Kevin has coached hundreds of people making a difference in Kansas communities. His work with senior teams is legendary, helping them break through what previously seemed impossible. I've learned a lot from him over the years, but nothing was more powerful than a simple one-liner he mentioned to me back in 2010. We were still in the early years of creating the Kansas Leadership Center. Kevin had become a key member of the team. Five or six of us were once again wrestling with a vexing issue that had frustrated everyone for months. The issue was about how KLC could and should reach Kansans across the political spectrum. As we were going round and round again, Kevin laid down the one liner:

"Ah, I see what's going on here. This is a classic case of unstated assumptions becoming premeditated resentments." There is so much wisdom in that line. With Kevin's help we eventually realized we were all operating under vastly different assumptions about the underlying issue. I thought making KLC a place where all Kansans, no matter their politics, felt at home was one of the two or three most important issues facing our organization. I believed if we failed on that issue, we would fail overall on our mission to build leadership at massive scale across Kansas. Everyone in that conversation agreed it was important. The question, we discovered, was *how* important? It was a top three issue for me. A top five issue for another. A top ten for another. And for one colleague it was important, but not more so than nineteen other things on her mind. While technically we all agreed it was important, it wasn't until we surfaced those differing assumptions that we could really begin to make progress.

These assumptions are alive for you too. Maybe you are a city council member, a school administrator, or a business executive. You care about Health. Of course you do! Who doesn't? Ask a crowd who is for Health and all hands will go up! But you also have assumptions about how important it is that you spend time on Health, what your role could be on Health, and who or what influences Health the most.

The people around you are in favor of Health too. City council members, school administrators, business executives, and others in authority are nearly unanimous in their support for Health. Some say the devil is in the details. Not me, the devil is in the assumptions. Our assumptions control us far more often than we control them.

Here's the basketball example again: an unstated assumption by Jack that the team couldn't score inside because of the other team's height could result in Jack taking more outside shots himself instead of passing to a teammate inside. That might create resentment in his teammate, who thought Jack was not passing to him because he didn't trust him.

If we aren't thoughtful about our assumptions, we run the risk of creating those "premeditated resentments" as we work to close The Health Gap.

In the nonprofit example above, board members are resentful that board meetings only scratch the surface. Eventually it's hard to get a quorum and frustration grows for all involved.

In the corporate example above, employees become resentful because they never hear their CEO talk about or ask about one of the most pressing concerns in their workforce, mental health. They begin to resent the CEO for being out of touch and aloof. The culture suffers, stress increases, and mental health challenges get worse.

In the state legislator example, advocates resent the legislator for "not caring" about Health. The resentment grows into disdain and contributes to polarization.

When have you had an example like this? If you are like me, probably more often than you care to admit. I was in a recent meeting about the disastrous groundwater contamination issue in northeast Wichita. The meeting was contentious and was nearly as disastrous as the contamination! The meeting involved city, county, and state officials and several other high-powered people. The 30,000 were well represented. And the two-hour meeting wasn't productive at all. The core problem with the meeting was that everyone had vastly different assumptions on everything from the purpose of the meeting to who should be involved to how to solve the groundwater problem.

Here's a leadership pro tip for those in authority: Use your authority to help others name their assumptions. When people realize they hold different assumptions than others, they are often good at figuring out how to move forward. But when they have no idea they hold different assumptions? At best, you get little progress, and at worst, you get chaos.

Our assumptions are often an invisible force pushing and pulling us in directions that often aren't useful. Closing The Health Gap requires a lot more of us to see this force. We need to control our assumptions, rather than let them control us.

When it comes to closing The Health Gap, the 30,000 must reset their assumptions specifically related to the who, what, and when.

First Big Assumption: You Know *Who* Needs to Be Involved

The first assumption that must be reset is about who needs to do what to ensure Kansans get Healthier. In a technical problem, an expert or authority does the work. The doctor sets the bone. The surgeon removes the tumor. The radiologist administers the chemotherapy. The Health Gap isn't a technical problem, but a lot of us think it is and assume it's mainly the work of the health care or public health community. It's not. Those experts have a part to play, but so do non-expert authorities (that's the 30,000) and stakeholders (that's all of us!). A lot of us also think Health is an individual issue. It is, once the playing field is level!

To oversimplify, any situation or challenge has three key groups: experts, authorities, and stakeholders. The assumptions we make about what those groups should do (or not do) are different depending on whether the situation is technical or adaptive.

In a technical problem, like the broken bone or tumor example, here's what's needed from each of those groups:

Experts: Solve the problem.

Stakeholders: Stay out of the way. Be patient.

Authorities: Give experts resources (time, money, space, etc.) to solve the problem. And calm stakeholders' fears.

But in adaptive challenges, like significantly increasing the number of insured Kansans, reducing occupational fatalities, reducing Black infant mortality, or climbing to number one in the Health rankings, what's needed from each group is very different. It looks more like this:

Experts: Share and analyze data, produce knowledge, and share or create best practices.

Stakeholders: Hold authorities accountable for focusing enough energy on the problems. Take ownership over the parts of the problem stakeholders must own.

Authorities: Raise the heat on the system. Disclose the problems. Protect those who share hard truths. Bring experts, other authorities, and stakeholders together to wrestle with the problems in a collaborative fashion. Remove barriers so stakeholders can do their part.

In an adaptive challenge, the role of expertise is limited. The foremost expert on public health might feel strongly about what should happen. She might have evidence to back that up. But she can't literally implement the policies needed.

Individuals need to take the walk, eat the apple, and get their annual checkup. Managers and CEOs need to create Health-friendly organizational policies. Policymakers need to adopt Health-friendly laws and regulations. (By the way, there are conservative and progressive ways of doing that. Don't mistake your preferences as the only way forward.)

Authorities—like the 30,000—can't force individuals to adopt Healthy behaviors but can make sure those behaviors are within reach for all individuals, families, and communities. The 30,000 have an outsized influence on whether we go for walks. They decide where there are sidewalks, crosswalks, bike lanes, etc. in our communities. Have you ever tried to walk across the intersection of Rock Road and Central in Wichita? Or 119th and Metcalf in Overland Park? Good luck getting across all those lanes without a police escort! Or, have you ever experienced how frightful it is to ride a bike on a rural county road when cars pass? The 30,000 are the ones who decide whether there should be wide shoulders on the road. That decision, like a lot of the decisions of the 30,000, affects Health. Here are some more examples:

The 30,000 have outsized influence on the air we breathe. They decide whether we encourage more dense development, which makes mass transit viable, thus improving air quality.

People should eat fresh food with an emphasis on fruits, vegetables, and lean protein. But the 30,000 usually decide where to locate businesses that sell that kind of food.

Parents should read to their children, giving them a boost in learning. But the 30,000 decide how we'll teach reading in schools and what level of failure or success is acceptable.

People should drink more water. But the 30,000 get to decide how much to invest in water quality. Or whether to fully disclose water contamination issues.

I could go on. You get it. To close The Health Gap, the 30,000 need to help everyone—experts, stakeholders, and other authorities—reset assumptions about who needs to do what to ensure Kansans are Healthy and that our state thrives.

Second Big Assumption: You Know *What* Needs to be Done

The second assumption that must be reset is about the type of work needed to close The Health Gap. In a technical problem, the attitude of the person doing the work needs to be one of confidence. They know they have the skills. They know how to use the skills. They are the right person for the job, and they know it. The doctor knows he can set the bone. The surgeon knows she can remove the tumor. In these situations, the work is exact.

In adaptive work, the attitude of those exercising leadership needs to be one of curiosity. It's not that they lack confidence. But their confidence is different. They are confident that if they stay curious, ask the right questions, engage the right people, challenge their own assumptions, and discover the right common ground, progress will result. They are confident because they are curious, and they know the challenge demands curiosity. In these situations, the work is exploratory.

In a technical problem, the work is all about efficiency and precision. Precisely set the bone. Get the cancer into remission. In adaptive challenges, the work is about investigation and experimentation. You are trying to figure out answers to key questions like: What interventions will work to close The Health Gap? Of those, which are possible given our civic and political context? Who should champion which interventions? How do we measure progress? Who needs to be involved? Who else?

Adaptive work is all about learning. Technical work is about executing what you've already learned. When my dad had a series of brain surgeries to treat his Parkinson's disease, the last thing our family wanted was the surgeon to be experimental. We wanted and expected a highly trained expert who would channel his knowledge into each of four half-day surgeries. We wanted efficiency and certainty.

Paradoxically, striving for those same things—efficiency and certainty—in the adaptive challenge of The Health Gap will make the gap a gulf. Read that sentence again and sit with it for a while.

Third Big Assumption: You Know *When* a Fix Should Fix Something (QUICK!)

In a technical problem, we want the work done as fast as possible. Set the bone fast. Get the cancer into remission as soon as possible. Progress on adaptive challenges requires patience and a longer time horizon. I've predicted it will take fifteen years for Kansas to lead the nation in Health and close The Health Gap. Exercising leadership in a situation like this looks like helping people hold steady, staying the course, celebrating the wins, and staying in the game through any setbacks.

In a technical problem, we should expect something to be solved. Your child will once again walk, run, and play when the bone heals. The tumor hopefully won't come back. In adaptive work, we should expect progress. On the one hand, we need to believe we can solve the challenge, that The Health Gap can be eliminated, and that we can lead the nation in Health. On the other hand, we need to understand that progress will take time. We want to eliminate The Health Gap, but should celebrate when it shrinks, and then get back to work to shrink it further.

We long for quick fixes. Sometimes they come around. A vaccine is a quick fix. But there's no overall vaccine for closing The Health Gap. Rather than one shot improving Health, it takes thousands of actions from thousands of individuals and organizations. Yes, it will take the modernization of our behavioral health practices and policies, but it will also take more walkable and environmentally friendly neighborhoods and cities. Yes, it will take private sector innovation regarding pharmaceuticals, but it will also take infrastructure for basic Health-related research. Yes, it will take new markets to provide unprocessed, fresh, and affordable food to all, but it will also take appropriate regulations to ensure the overall food supply contributes to Health.

It's tempting to position your preferred idea as a solution or even the quick fix for The Health Gap. But you should know better. Please understand, and help others understand, that your idea is just one piece of the puzzle. The danger with presenting, explicitly or implicitly, something as a quick fix is two-fold.

First, it crowds out energy on other necessary pieces of the puzzle. See the Medicaid expansion debate in Kansas over the last decade as an example. I can't help but wonder if the advocates for expansion, myself included, have been so focused on that one piece of the puzzle that we may have lacked focus on other critical pieces.

Second, it can demoralize your people if your "fix" is enacted and The Health Gap remains. Back to the Medicaid expansion example, there have been times I have likely described

Medicaid expansion as a quick fix for everything related to The Health Gap. It's not. Even with expansion, the gap would remain, although it might be smaller.

Use Your Authority to Help Others Name Their Assumptions about Improving Health

This is what it could look like:

While discussing the twin problems of increasing health premiums and employees taking more sick leave, a CEO uses her authority to have her executive team name the assumptions they hold about how to improve Health in the company.

During a town hall meeting about Health, an elected official uses her authority to ask the audience about their assumptions related to improving Health, and she shares her own too.

At a retreat with his cabinet, a bishop creates space for his top advisors to discuss their assumptions about the role of the church in closing The Health Gap.

Here are four tactics that the CEO, elected official, or bishop could use in those settings. (And these will work for you, too, in your organization, community, or company.)

- **After asking people to name their assumptions about the adaptive challenge, use your authority to facilitate a conversation around two questions:** 1) How might these assumptions help us make progress? 2) How might these assumptions get in the way of progress? The point is to disrupt the certainty people have in their heads and hearts. With adaptive work you often need to disrupt the narrative and create conditions for a more open, creative, and exploratory conversation.

- **Help people create a list for what the work looks like for experts, stakeholders, and authorities.** This will help them see the complexities of the work and the need to ensure we focus on everyone doing their part.

- **Exactness and precision or curiosity and exploration?** When working on any of the issues that connect to Health (e.g., substance abuse, affordable housing, reducing childhood trauma, insuring more people, etc.) create a discussion around this question: "Does this issue call more for exactness and precision or curiosity and exploration? Why?" It will, of course, need both. But the more adaptive the issue—and The Health Gap is full of adaptive issues—the more the discussion should lead to the latter not the former.

- **Facilitate the creation of a "progress timeline".**
  Ask, "If we enact that policy (or launch that initiative, or make that change, etc.), what do we honestly think the result will be on Health? In the next twelve months? Five years? Ten years?" This usually helps people see two things. First, how their preferred idea to improve Health doesn't solve as much of the underlying problem as they want to believe. Second, that closing The Health Gap will always take longer than we care to admit.

Exercising leadership is always about working the issues behind the issue! The issue we are discussing in this book is Health. But our assumptions about Health are some of the issues behind the issue. We won't make progress on Health without naming our assumptions and evolving them to ensure they help us make progress rather than lock us in place.

It's a leadership challenge because
It Requires Loss

This chapter is going to be a rough one for some of you to read, especially those of you who have (or had) a lot of authority on the topic of Health in Kansas. Before I get to the gut punches, let me explain some important ideas about leadership.

First, leadership doesn't happen often. It's rare. It's the exception, not the rule. This is totally obvious if you operate with my definition of leadership: leadership is mobilizing others to make progress on daunting challenges. That is a high bar and most of us don't clear it often. I've worked for years to mobilize major progress on the number of uninsured Kansans. The numbers aren't improving much. I've clearly failed to exercise leadership on that issue. Trying hard doesn't count as "leadership." It counts as, well, trying. And that's fine, but let's not confuse trying with leading.

Second, those best at exercising leadership only get it right occasionally. It's like baseball. The best hitters in the league, or even the best hitters of all time, still fail more than they succeed. My experience is that the numbers are similar in leadership. The best of the best successfully mobilize progress on a daunting challenge maybe every three attempts out of ten. Challenges—like closing The Health Gap—are daunting for a reason. If progress were easy, the challenges wouldn't be around. We might not like admitting that we fail at exercising leadership more than we succeed, but it's illogical to think otherwise.

Third, it's hard for people like you—someone in authority— to exercise leadership because you often get rewarded for doing otherwise. (Read a few more lines before you slam this book shut.) Those in authority—CEOs, cabinet secretaries, executive directors, etc.—usually get rewarded for things running smoothly, for there being no big hiccups, and for things never quite getting chaotic. That's good. We need organizations that can function. But exercising leadership, on Health or other topics, is always about disruption. And we all know what happens to a senior authority figure who creates too much disruption! We've all seen those oh so fast transitions to becoming a "consultant" as they look for their next job. All that pressure to keep things smooth makes it hard for someone in authority to do anything too disruptive. But leadership requires disruption. See the paradox?

Here's where things could feel hard for those of you who have significant formal authority that directly connects to Health. I don't think it should feel hard, but I understand it might. Exercising leadership is always about change. It's hard to say there's much leadership happening if things in your organization, community, or state are pretty much staying the same or getting worse. To be blunt, it's hard to say there is enough leadership happening on Health in Kansas when we've fallen from #8 to #29. And I don't believe that is the fault of those who are in senior authority roles in our traditional health organizations. I know so many cabinet secretaries, hospital CEOs, and nonprofit executive directors who have dedicated their lives to serving their organization and our state. I don't put the blame on those authorities. I put it on the 30,000, myself included, for not understanding our connection to improving Health in Kansas.

When talking with Kansans about The Health Gap I often hear the line, "People are afraid of change." That is, of course, totally false. People are okay with change, so long as it is change they like. They like a 300% boost to their department budget. They like winning a $1 billion lottery ticket. They like being given the opportunity to implement changes *they* dreamed up. People like a weight loss drug that doesn't require any work. People like surgeries that are shorter because of new technologies. People like receiving more employee benefits at work. People are fine with change, per se.

It's a loss people don't like. People resist change they think isn't good for them.

A manager would love for her team to be Healthier and experience more well-being but isn't willing to lose the current "we work more hours each week than any other team" mindset that she instilled in her culture. A county commissioner would love to have a comprehensive solution to preventing and treating homelessness but doesn't want to raise taxes or cut existing funding to get it. A state senator would love to have fewer uninsured Kansans but is unwilling to give up something he is very proud about: Kansas's position as one of the few remaining states not to expand Medicaid. Believing the "people are afraid of change" mantra allows that manager, county commissioner, and senator to blame others in their situation and let themselves off the hook. It diminishes their own agency.

What Is the Real or Perceived Loss Associated with Closing The Health Gap

We won't climb the rankings and improve Health without a whole lot of change, including the kind that will create real or perceived loss. A very uncomfortable interpretation about why the Health of Kansas continues to slide is that we—the 30,000—have been unable or unwilling to help our people understand and accept the loss that comes with progress. These losses include:

- **Loss of innocence.** Centering on the Health rankings will make it harder to assume we are winning when we are, in fact, losing. Keeping the rankings in front of us will make it harder to celebrate that new program or initiative that we *think* will improve Health. We'll still celebrate it, but we will be more tempered, because success is about actually improving Health, not the shiny new program or initiative. We'll lose the ability to feel warm and fuzzy about *our* shiny new thing.

- **Loss of ability to go it alone.** If we are serious about climbing the rankings we are going to have to work together more. The state Health foundations will need to engage in deep collaboration, rather than the occasional coordination. The fifty nonprofits working on early literacy in south-central Kansas (I'm not joking. That number is real!) will need to collaborate, converge, or even combine! Some of the myriads of Health coalitions across Kansas could need to combine, join forces, and focus together. For example, does Wichita need a Health and Wellness Coalition, a Mental Health and Substance Abuse Coalition, a Continuum of Care Coalition for Homelessness, etc.? Maybe so. But perhaps not. Not everything should be combined. But not everything should be separate either. Nobody thinks of themselves as someone who loves silos. But most of us end up working in silos.

- **Loss of loyalty to your preferred strategy.** We've been debating Medicaid expansion for almost a decade. Medicaid expansion is a strategy and happens to be one I prefer. Health savings accounts are a strategy too. Those and many other health-related efforts of the last twenty years are strategies, not goals. Leading the nation in Health is a goal, and a quite specific and ambitious one. We know that if we can help enough of the 30,000 become loyal to the goal of leading the nation in Health, their preferred strategies will still be important to them but should be less so. But letting go of their preferred strategies could feel like a loss to them.

- **Loss of ability to prioritize everything.** We are experiencing a lot of loss at The Kansas Health Foundation. To have more impact on Health, we know we must simplify our efforts. That means we are now saying no to things we would love to say yes to, but simply can't. Saying yes is fun. It makes people happy, especially when you are an endowed foundation giving away money! But we know simplicity is a key to more impact. That means we are investing more in fewer partners. It's a good change, but there is real loss involved. A lot of organizations are frustrated with us. That doesn't feel good. It feels like a loss to us. And then there is the monetary loss those organizations we used to support are feeling as we've focused resources elsewhere.

- **Loss of opportunity.** Anytime you use your authority and leadership to help people focus on one thing, you create the loss of opportunity to focus on other things. I know that is at play with the message of this book and the 30,000. Improving Health will require us to invest more time, energy, and resources to move the fifty plus measures in the Health rankings. That's time, energy, and resources not going to other things. There are plenty of important topics our state could focus on that don't show up in those Health measures, things like tourism, oil and gas exploration, financial literacy, childcare, and many more. Each of you reading this book likely has one or more things you care deeply about and want to advance. For many of you, what I am asking you to do—focus on the Health rankings rather than your preferred issue— will feel like a loss. My hope is that, in time, you'll see it more as a refocusing and reprioritizing. Your work is indirectly, if not directly, connected to the rankings.

Four things to keep in mind as you navigate change and loss:

See Resistance to Your Change Initiative as Data Rather than a Problem

I used to think there was a simple solution if someone was resisting my wonderful, smart, perfect change initiative I would simply talk louder! I would say it again, with more volume, more passion, and maybe even with some rhetorical devices that make it harder for them to resist (at least in the moment). I might say something like, "So, would you like to join this perfectly thought-out plan or continue to align yourself with the bad ideas of the past?"

But over time I learned the resistance to my bright ideas is useful. It points me in the direction of what the loss might be with my big idea. Once I know that, I can try to mitigate that loss as much as possible.

Closing The Health Gap will create resistance. We need to understand that, so we can mitigate the loss as much as possible. When Kansas reformed laws about smoking indoors in restaurants, advocates needed to appreciate that restaurant and bar owners were afraid of losing money and potentially their businesses. When primary care physicians are mandated to screen for more conditions, advocates need to appreciate that these doctors will fear losing the ability to decide for themselves how they spend their precious few minutes with each patient. When businesses are forced to cover more health care costs, advocates need to appreciate that many business executives fear losing the ability to afford the health care coverage they already offer employees.

Progress on adaptive challenges requires adaptation and letting go. It requires the type of change that involves loss. Resistance from others tells us what loss our bright ideas might be creating. One of the biggest mistakes people make when exercising leadership is being clueless about the losses they are asking others to take for the sake of progress.

Speak to Loss

Once you know the loss or losses your change effort will create, you can help others get ready or even mitigate those losses. Rather than sweep the loss (or perceived loss) under the rug, use your authority to focus attention on the losses. Those skilled at exercising leadership know that "speaking to loss" creates energy and momentum for progress. It's paradoxical, but true.

A business official wanting to create a Healthier workforce faces resistance to her reforms from senior managers worried about productivity. She should empathetically and consistently acknowledge those concerns when talking about her proposals, even if she doesn't believe her reforms will reduce productivity. She must acknowledge their concerns.

A governor advocating for massive investment in early care and education faces resistance from other advocates connected to other social issues. They want the same focus on their issue. The governor in this situation should also empathetically and consistently acknowledge those concerns. She has prioritized early care and education at the expense of other issues. That's factual and speaking directly to that, rather than pretending it's not true, will actually and paradoxically create energy and momentum.

People are energized when they feel and experience someone in authority who understands their loss and frustration and is willing to name it.

Let Loss Speak

You can also use your authority to create the conditions for others to speak up about the loss they are feeling or fearing.

Again, it's paradoxical, but doing this will create energy and momentum for progress! Here are a couple examples:

A public official could hold a town meeting on a difficult subject and use the forum not to speak to the people, but to let the people speak to her.

An advocate for reform could ask, with sincere curiosity, what opponents of his ideas believe will happen if his reforms are enacted. And rather than defend and explain, he could simply listen and learn. I'm not saying he should change his mind (although we should be willing to make a new decision based on new information). But simply inviting opponents to speak their truth helps energize progress.

This idea of "letting loss speak" is why I love the question: What concerns you the most? I ask that question whenever I'm pushing a new idea or project. Knowing what concerns people the most is a window into the real or perceived loss they might experience if my great idea comes to fruition. Asking that question almost always leads to a good conversation. And good conversations add energy to change.

Take Some Losses Yourself

The norm is for people in authority to engage in ways that lead to all upside for their people. And if there needs to be loss, the loss ends up with the other guys. But that norm is a recipe for the status quo on deep, daunting adaptive challenges like Health. Leadership on Health is about understanding the real or perceived loss, speaking to that loss, and letting that loss speak. But it's also about intervening—especially for those in authority—in ways that distribute the losses as much as possible.

Our exhausting decade-long debate in Kansas about Medicaid expansion is the perfect example of this idea. The political context makes it obvious that expansion—or some other strategy to reduce the number of uninsured Kansans (remember, expanding Medicaid is simply a strategy, the goal is dramatically more Kansans with quality insurance)—will only occur if the different political factions each gain something. That likely means each faction will need to lose something too. That's how progress works on things like this. Leadership here isn't browbeating the opposition. It's giving the opposition enough of a win so they can stomach the loss. It's co-creating a strategy to help each relevant faction get a win, which will make the loss more tenable for their people, who will likely be upset about the losses that come with the deal.

Ironically, I feel the need to speak to the loss I may have created with this chapter. For many of you, a heavy chapter about loss isn't your cup of tea. You might crave energy and optimism, and this chapter could feel like a downer and too pessimistic. I simply ask you to consider two things.

First, the next time you are pushing a big change, lean into the loss you could be creating rather than avoid it. I know it might not feel good at first, but I promise you it's the key to unlocking energy and enthusiasm. Remember, the odds are against you when attempting to mobilize people to make progress on daunting challenges like Health. The most likely outcome is the status quo. You don't want that. Many of your people probably don't either. But it's what you and they will get unless confronted and provoked into new ways of thinking. Exercising leadership by leaning into the loss will be experienced as new, different, and provocative. The very things you'll need to get a result that is beyond the status quo.

Second, remember that the relationship between loss and progress isn't new. I'm not breaking ground here. It's the oldest pattern in the universe. Everything is in a constant cycle of birth, death, and resurrection. If the word "resurrection" is too spiritual for you, replace it with re-creation or re-use. The tree leaves sprout. The flowers bloom. Eventually they die. There is loss. This pattern is true in nature, us, and our work. It's also true for massive challenges like Health. It's a paradox, and those skilled at exercising leadership understand that progress almost always involves paradox. A "paradox" happens when two or more things that seem contradictory are, upon deeper inspection, illuminating a truth. Here are some key paradoxes that are often alive when working on tough issues: Go slow to go fast. Less is more. Simplicity can be complicated. Conflict is often needed for peace or progress. We often need to endure pain to achieve meaningful change. For instance, the passage of clean indoor air laws caused significant backlash initially but has since become a monumental public health victory that no one frets about any longer.

Those skilled at exercising leadership on Health must be comfortable with another paradox:

To win we must lose.

We close The Health Gap by accepting loss and helping others do the same. The loss is worth it because the gain—closing The Health Gap—is one of the most purposeful and good things we can do with our authority. When someone has been given much, they should be able to take losses for the greater good. I'm not talking about "time, talent, and treasure" here. I'm trying to make it as clear as possible that leading Health is about letting go more than holding on, about adapting our perspective more than holding firm, about mitigating loss more than almost anything else.

CHAPTER 10

It's a leadership challenge because
It's Risky

I served in the legislature right before starting the Kansas
Leadership Center. That's likely one of the reasons why
"leadership is risky" is one of the five principles taught in
all KLC programs. Progress on all adaptive challenges is
risky. Risk is baked into the situation. We'll explore what
the risk is related to The Health Gap in a bit. But for now,
you need to know that the risk associated with exercising
leadership on an adaptive challenge is the big reason why
people don't exercise leadership very often.

Leadership is risky because it's about disruption. People
would rather not be disrupted. Remember, people are okay
with good change, but not change that messes up their
world (or that they perceive will mess up their world).
That type of change is experienced as disruption. People
don't like that. A lot of people are okay with other people
being disrupted. Some are even okay with causing that
disruption for others. But experience disruption ourselves?
Nope. Nada. No thank you. The risk of exercising leadership
is glossed over in most leadership development efforts.
Or it's replaced with a "leadership is lonely" idea, which is
accurate, but also not quite the same idea.

There has been an explosion of youth leadership programs in Kansas and beyond over the last twenty years. Schools, colleges, public clubs, and many other organizations have started offering leadership programs and courses. More young people come of age with an understanding that anyone can lead, anytime, anywhere. I love it. But I worry that many of those programs avoid some of the harsh realities— the risk involved—that come with exercising leadership.

For example, national fraternities now invest tens of millions annually in leadership programming for their members. The training is interesting and even inspiring. But the focus often is on ambiguous leadership concepts (i.e., inspire a collective purpose!) and revolves around a battery of personality assessments (i.e., Meyers Briggs, DiSC Profile, True Colors, etc.). That's all fine and good, but shouldn't we more specifically prepare young people for the risk they'll face if they attempt to exercise leadership at their university to eliminate hazing?

A friend of mine participated in every leadership opportunity imaginable growing up: 4H, student government in middle and high school, a church leadership camp, a minor in leadership studies at Kansas State University, and countless other "leadership" activities. And then she wound up in the Kansas Legislature. I remember her sharing how leading in the state government was nothing like all her past "leadership" experiences. In the capitol, you need sharp elbows and thick skin. It's not fun and games, but hard, intense, and full of risk. What's the risk? Remember, leadership is about disrupting things. Do that slightly wrong in politics and you might not serve in the government very long.

But progress on adaptive challenges like Health require disruption. Things will keep getting worse if we don't disrupt things. The trajectory of Kansas is predictable without more disruption. Kansas will continue to slide in the Health rankings. And that slide will be a proxy for an overall slide in our state's quality of life, economic competitiveness, and people's happiness. Disruption is required.

The challenge is that disruption is rarely rewarded, as we explored in the last chapter. Keep the staff and board happy and a nonprofit executive can have many years in the position without anyone asking too many questions about whether progress has been made on their underlying mission. Keep shareholders happy with a decent annual return and a corporate CEO can avoid the need to orchestrate the disruption that might be needed to elevate the company to the next level. A foundation executive can keep everyone happy by continuing to fund the projects and organizations the foundation has always funded. Thus, avoiding the angst that would come with disrupting funding patterns. However, those disruptions might be exactly what is needed to propel progress on the issues the foundation cares most about.

Some of the 30,000, especially those of us who serve in elected office, get rewarded for disrupting the "other". That might mean western Kansas legislators getting rewarded by their constituents for "sticking it" to the folks in Johnson

County and vice versa. Or it might mean Republicans being rewarded for disrupting a Democratic governor's plans. But that type of disruption is easy. The challenge comes when you need to disrupt your own people. Which leads to my favorite definition of leadership. I heard it first from Marty Linsky, now my dear friend, mentor, and grandfather-like figure to my kids. But when I first heard this statement, Marty was just a provocative speaker at the front of a room in which I was in the audience. And provoke me he did. Here's his definition of leadership:

"Leadership is disappointing your own people at a rate they can absorb."

Meditate on that line for a few minutes if you are serious about helping to close The Health Gap. It perfectly describes why leadership is risky and why it hardly ever happens.

What's Risky about Leading The Health Gap

It's risky for an executive in a food retail business to raise questions about a correlation between his company products—all of which are high in preservatives, sugar, and fat—and the fact that Kansans are becoming less Healthy. It's risky for an employee to question why physical health seems to be respected in her company but not so much mental health. It's risky for a conservative elected official to give a speech about how we all contribute to the Health of one another and about how we need to do more collectively to support Health. It's risky for a progressive activist to write a column challenging advocacy organizations to see conservative policymakers in Kansas as partners rather than enemies.

I feel at risk in writing this book and casting this vision for Kansas to lead the nation in Health. There really isn't much related to Health I can literally control in Kansas. The Kansas Health Foundation is pretty small compared to the scale of the problem. And so much of Kansans' Health is influenced by national and global trends. It would be safer to cast a smaller vision. Instead of leading the nation, how about just improving our place in the Health rankings? To be even less risky we could have just stuck with our existing mission statement "to improve the Health of all Kansans". It's a feel-good statement. We really do want to improve the Health of all Kansans. It's true. But it's also pretty risk-free because measuring the Health of every single Kansan is hard to do.

What's the risk for me about our audacious purpose to help Kansas lead the nation in Health? Imagine we don't move up in the rankings. Even if it can be explained due to national factors or something, do you think I will be in this role very long? Being bold is risky.

When we lead Health initiatives, we risk setting ourselves and others up for disappointing results, because it is so hard to close The Health Gap. There's also the risk of your own people—in your company, political faction, organization, or professional field—getting frustrated with you. Because if you are leading, you'll be helping them discover their piece of the mess. You'll be disrupting the narrative, the story in their heads, that allows them to put their head on the pillow at night and see themselves as a hero in their do-good story (or at the very least not a villain!).

All of this connects to reputational risk. You and I are quite skilled at subconsciously avoiding all sorts of things that could damage our precious ego. Which leads to a unique dynamic about risk and The Health Gap:

When it comes to closing The Health Gap, there is a mismatch between who takes on the risk and who gains from that risk.

Improving Health is the type of situation where the people for whom leading is risky (that's you and me) have a lot to lose and, frankly, not much to personally gain. Our Health is already pretty good. Most of the 30,000 don't face the inequities and barriers that are fueling The Health Gap. Closing The Health Gap in Kansas, helping Kansas climb the rankings, isn't likely to impact our Health too much. Because of the financial stability and the privilege that comes with our authority, we tend to be some of the Healthiest people around. In fact, as Health in Kansas has continued to slide for the last thirty years, the Health of people like us has likely just gotten better and better. We could deduce as much from Michael Marmot's research, which I mentioned in Chapter 2, about the connection between social standing and longevity.

We have access to more pharmaceuticals and clinical treatments than ever before. We are more likely to live in neighborhoods that are conducive for walking and exercise. We also are more likely to have the financial resources to belong to a gym and to purchase fitness clothes, shoes, and equipment for our homes. Almost all of the 30,000 have employer-provided health insurance and can take time off work if they are sick or need to go to the doctor. Our financial situation leads to better Health. Here's a personal example: Twice over the last year I've been frustrated when trying to find a provider that I liked and that my insurance would cover. Early in the year I was looking for a therapist. Later I was looking for a physical therapist. I quickly pivoted and stopped looking for providers that would be covered by my insurance. I was willing to pay 100% out-of-pocket if I found providers that I liked. The result? I received high-quality care quickly. I felt better faster. My therapist helped me work through some mental health challenges with minimal disruption to my work and family life. My physical therapist helped my shoulder heal and got me back to my workouts, which have always anchored my physical and mental health. Talk about privilege!

What Helps People Take On the Risk of Leading Health

- **Know how The Health Gap affects what you care about.** Game-changing things happen when people care so much about something—their family, community, organization, and employees—that they are willing to take real risk to bring about progress. While The Health Gap might not be making your Health worse, it is affecting you. For example, I serve on the board of the Greater Wichita Partnership, a high-performing organization that cares deeply about growing the Wichita economy. My fellow board members and I need to understand that the persistent increase in The Health Gap in Wichita is a drag on our ability to compete with places like Kansas City, Tulsa, and Denver.

- **Make leadership skills ubiquitous.** Effective leadership mitigates risk. That's often the whole point of exercising leadership. There is something important that needs to be done. It's not getting done because people don't like the risks of disruption and loss that will come with the change. The people who mobilize things to bring about the change are the ones who can effectively mitigate the risk enough for others to join in. The more people who have these skills the better. More people leading equals lower risk for all involved. And that gets you more progress.

Leading Health is risky. Progress will require disruption and loss. We'll need to do plenty of that "disrupting our own people at a rate they can absorb" stuff. Sometimes we won't get the rate exactly right. We'll go too far and really frustrate people. Other times we won't go far enough, and nothing will happen. But I believe there will eventually be enough of the 30,000 who will understand how to intervene and mobilize action to close The Health Gap in Kansas. Along the way, we will experience the risk of leading. That risk will cause our own people to sometimes question us, think we are wrong, say we are not ready to lead, or worse, believe that we are ill-equipped for our job. To those scenarios I say, "Who cares?" Let's be okay with a little friendly fire from people who are likely already experiencing good Health. Lead well, and those people will get over it, eventually. Accept the risk that comes with leading Health and real change will come to those suffering the most because of The Health Gap.

CHAPTER 11

It's a leadership challenge because
Authority
Isn't Enough

Part Two of this book has explored several reasons why making progress in Health is a leadership challenge, not a Health challenge. The issues brought up in Part Two— loss, faulty assumptions, inability to create agreement on the problem let alone the solutions, risk for those who attempt to lead—are ever-present characteristics for almost any daunting challenge. You can find those issues alive in debates from education reform to artificial intelligence regulation. Closer to home, these issues are alive all over Kansas. They exist as Wichita continues to try to diversify its economy to be less reliant on aviation. As Western Kansas attempts to create an economic future without the Ogallala Aquifer. And as Johnson and Wyandotte Counties attempt to create an amazing school experience for all kids, no matter what side of the county line they call home. The details change, but the high-level issues are almost always the same. Those skilled at exercising leadership know this and focus their energy on understanding and mitigating the issues I've explored here in Part Two.

But there's one more issue that needs to be mentioned, one more dynamic that makes it clear that closing The Health Gap and helping Kansas lead the nation in Health is a leadership challenge, not a Health challenge. Here it is:

Authority isn't enough.

I will close Part Two of this book with this short chapter on the topic of your authority. I know my talk of authority versus leadership can feel cumbersome for some of you. Some of you think it's easier and more convenient to just refer to those with authority (e.g., CEOs, executive directors, boards of directors, cabinet secretaries, elected officials, corporate senior teams, etc.) as the "leaders." But after creating the Kansas Leadership Center and coaching thousands of people in senior positions, I know that conflating leadership with authority slows progress on the biggest issues, like Health.

Think of it this way: Given the fact that Kansas has been declining in Health since the 1990s, shouldn't we question current norms? One of the norms that must be questioned is how we think about leadership and authority.

Your authority, assuming you use it correctly, can solve a lot of problems. A business owner can put the right people in the right spots in her company. A city manager can pressure a police chief to evolve the department's practices to include more community policing. A legislator can use their authority to get a state agency to respond to a question from a constituent. Those of you who control budgets can use that authority to solve things too. A chief operating officer can adjust a budget to increase insurance benefits for employees. A school superintendent can shift resources to allow for the hiring of more tutors to help students at risk of failing. A pastor can decide to invest more in the church's hunger outreach ministry.

But no one person or one organization has enough authority to solve The Health Gap in Kansas.

It's another reason why this is a leadership challenge, not a Health challenge. Leadership is always about mobilizing others—usually others you can't control—to work on and make progress on a daunting challenge.

Here's a way of thinking about it: You know you have a leadership challenge on your hands when there are literally people in authority who know what should be done but can't make it happen. In some ways, the overall Health challenge in Kansas mirrors the physician to patient dynamic. Every doctor, whether a family physician or a brain surgeon, knows behaviors and habits that will improve health in their patients. They can preach the need to exercise, stop smoking, only drink alcohol occasionally, etc. But those doctors (and all other health care practitioners) lack the authority to literally enact those behaviors. It's similar in public and private life.

The Kansas Department of Health and Environment (KDHE) oversees most public health efforts in Kansas as well as the state's Medicaid program. Every cabinet secretary of KDHE, from both Republican and Democratic administrations over the last thirty years could tell you evidence-based practices that could improve Health in Kansas. But none had enough authority on their own to enact all those practices.

Every county health officer, whether a Republican or a Democrat, a conservative or a progressive, knows initiatives that if implemented would improve Health in their counties. But none have enough authority alone to enact all those initiatives.

Most human resource professionals know a host of programs and practices that could lead to a Healthier workforce for their companies. But enacting these policies requires attention and resources from other departments. It is not under the authority of most HR professionals to demand that these changes take place in their companies.

Prior to starting the Kansas Leadership Center I served in the Kansas House of Representatives and prior to that I served as an aide to Governor Bill Graves. In both roles, especially the former but also the latter, I was often called a "leader". But the truth is that sometimes I exercised leadership and a lot of the time I didn't. Remember my definition of leadership is mobilizing others to make progress on daunting challenges. No one exercises leadership all the time. It's impossible. I knew that intuitively as I journeyed through my early career in public service. When I was thirty-one and starting the Kansas Leadership Center, I set out to become an expert on leadership. And because the norm was (and in too many instances still is) to conflate leadership with authority, I knew I had to become an expert on authority as well. I needed to help others see why they'll make more progress on what they care about if they stop conflating these two subjects. Here's a short summary of the differences between the two:

AUTHORITY ...	LEADERSHIP ...
is a role	is an activity
maintains the status quo	disrupts the status quo
provides direction	shakes things up
can show leadership	must come from all levels
calms things down	provides inspiration

Progress on closing The Health Gap requires a lot of authority and a lot of leadership. We need it all. And the 30,000 need to know that while we can't make progress just with them (with their authority), we certainly can't make progress without them doing their part. As we approach Part Three of this book, I need you to keep in mind what your authority can and can't do.

Your authority alone can't boost Kansas from #29 to #1 in the rankings. But we can't climb the rankings without you and others in authority doing your part. If you don't use your authority, if you don't do your part, it's likely that the slide of Health in Kansas will continue. But if you use your authority in the ways described in Part Three of this book, we can create the conditions necessary for game-changing progress.

That's the role of authority in adaptive work: Use your power, influence, and authority to create the conditions for transformative work among all the necessary stakeholders. That's what leadership looks like from those in authority. It's a limited, yet critical role. It's a role we need you to play and play well. Part Three shows you how.

Nine Mindsets to Close The Health Gap

Part One described the symptoms.
Part Two gave the diagnosis.
Part Three will give the prescription.

Let's recap the symptoms: Kansas used to be one of the Healthiest states in America. Now we are at the low end of the middle of the pack. We've been falling precipitously since the early 1990s. At #29, we are below average. This has a major impact on the ability of our state, communities, neighborhoods, organizations, and families to thrive. Everything from growing our economy to retaining our young people to improving our schools is harder because we are 29th. Kansans in authority—the 30,000—need a North Star to mobilize our attention and effort. America's Health Rankings are the right star to guide us, and if we don't start climbing the rankings, the future of Kansas will not be bright.

As I explored in Part Two, the diagnosis is counter intuitive. Yes, all of this is about Health and that's broadly understood. But digging deeper, I showed it's a leadership challenge *before* it's a Health challenge. You know it's a leadership challenge because there are plenty of experts who know what needs to be done but literally can't make those things happen.

Progress requires lots of people—especially the 30,000—to mobilize others to care more and do more to improve Health in Kansas. Mobilizing others will require helping people understand what's causing the slide and what might turn it around. The 30,000 will need to examine our existing assumptions and call those assumptions into question. Progress will require loss, or at least the perception of loss. And causing people to feel loss seems risky, especially to those in authority. Because those in authority can't supply all the effort needed for progress. Those in authority need to motivate others to get past the sense of loss so we can bridge The Health Gap. All the Health initiatives in the world will just tinker around the edges if Kansas doesn't solve for these dynamics.

That brings us to Part Three, the prescription. The ideas in this part of the book emerge from three sources: my personal experience in Kansas civic life, the collective wisdom of the Kansas Health Foundation (board of directors and staff), and the deep listening exercise I described in Part One. This book offers a roadmap for Kansas to close The Health Gap, climb the Health rankings and, eventually, lead the nation in Health. This roadmap isn't a detailed policy agenda, although it will take policy change. This roadmap isn't a step-by-step plan, as if one could be created anyway! The roadmap is a set of mindsets that must be held by enough of the 30,000 to give Kansas a chance at stopping the slide and starting the climb. Enough of the 30,000 manifesting the mindsets described in Part Three will lead to a multitude of policy and programmatic changes related to Health in the coming years. Those changes will create better Health outcomes. But we can't get to those outcomes without first adopting these nine mindsets.

CHAPTER 12

Mindset #1:
Work Upstream

Do we need charity or change? The answer, of course, is we need both. Getting the balance right is the challenge. By "charity" I mean efforts to alleviate pain and suffering now. By "change" I mean efforts to eliminate what caused the pain and suffering in the first place. Charity is good. Change is better. Charity is what's called "downstream" work in the civic and do-gooder fields. We need more "upstream" work. And we need you to champion an upstream mindset.

Charity is giving food to a hungry person, offering a place to sleep to a person who is homeless, or providing medical care to someone who needs it but can't afford it. Kansans pride themselves on our charitable hearts. It's baked into our DNA going back to the old days when everyone in a community turned out to help raise a barn. That charitable DNA is likely why Kansas ranks seventh among all states for volunteerism (it's one of the measures in America's Health Rankings). That's fabulous, but every strength can also be a vulnerability.

Most of us have taken multiple personality type assessments. My favorite is the Enneagram, an ancient tool that continues to provoke people to deeper discernment

today. What I love about the Enneagram is the clear understanding that what makes you special, powerful, and
valuable is the same thing that, depending on the situation
or context, can quickly become your greatest vulnerability.
If Kansas took the Enneagram, it would learn the dark side
of its charitable default. Charity weakens the impetus to
change the conditions that create the need for charity in the
first place.

To improve Health we must keep the charity coming but
also understand that it won't help us go from 29th to 1st.
It likely won't keep us at 29th either. It's a moral imperative
to care for the poor, the widows, and the orphans. Kansans
get that. The problem for the 30,000 and others who can
influence The Health Gap is that the charity work feels
good. It warms our hearts to help others and allows us to
tell ourselves a story where we are doing the good work
expected of us. And so we might feel our job is done
if we provide charity. But charity is "downstream" work.
And to stop the need for downstream work we need
more "upstream" work.

You've probably read this before, but the metaphor used to
explain "upstream" thinking is usually something like this:
Once upon a time there was a village along the bank of a
river. Villagers started to notice babies floating down the
river and quickly organized rescue efforts. They were saving
all the babies and were quite proud of their efforts. Tears
of joy would occur with every baby saved. After a while,
a well-designed system of rescue was in place, with various

people knowing their part in the system. The energy to create and maintain the rescue system kept mounting. But all agreed it was worth it. After all, they were saving babies! But there was a woman who had the ability to hold two thoughts in her head at once. She knew the rescue operation was important and must be sustained, but also had other thoughts running through her mind. One day, after ending her shift in the rescue operation, she left the village and started walking upriver. Her husband yelled after her, "Where are you going?" She replied, "I'm going upstream to stop whoever the heck is throwing babies into the river!"

There are many necessary downstream efforts when it comes to Health. Most health care is downstream work, just like the situation I described earlier in this book regarding my University of Kansas Hospital System experience. We can't stop treating those cancer patients, stabilizing those trauma victims, or saving those stroke patients. Except for preventive care, most health care happens, and most health care dollars get spent, once we are already sick. It's downstream work. In fact, the largest contracts in state government are for Medicaid, the state/federal health insurance program for the poor, which is predominantly downstream work. There are so many other downstream efforts, such as food pantries, criminal justice programs, (most) foster care situations, and many more opportunities that consume our nonprofit, civic, faith, and community organizations.

We need to keep doing all these things. There are a lot of babies that need saving! But we also need people to head upriver and stop whoever is putting the babies in the river in the first place. And heading upriver is different and disruptive. It's not the norm. It's provocative and might be misunderstood. "How dare you neglect these babies in the river!" Remember, in the story everyone was preoccupied playing their part to keep the current system running (to keep saving the babies). It's a silly example, but we can imagine the courage and commitment it must have taken from the woman who decided to head upriver.

I've noticed an interesting dynamic in Kansas. When people who are already Healthy become more concerned about The Health Gap, they tend to gravitate toward downstream efforts. They want to make sure the homeless have shelter, the hungry have a sandwich, or the battered woman has a safe place for her and her children to live. Most of the charity galas I've attended focus on this downstream mind-set. That's fine. There is nothing wrong with that per se. In fact, there is a lot right with it. We need to keep all that downstream work happening. But well-meaning people tend to default to where they can make the quickest difference. That usually leads to charity. But charity treats problems rather than solving them. It's an exercise of leadership to honor the commitment and contributions of this charity work while at the same time calling people to also engage in upstream work. That's an exercise of leadership.

What It Looks Like to Hold an Upstream Mindset

- **A pastor** who has been on the front lines of encouraging people to adopt foster kids, dedicates a four-part sermon series to exploring changes society and the church should consider so fewer kids would enter foster care in the first place.

- **An executive director** of a nonprofit that works with kids in foster care, creates a coalition of private businesses to ensure mothers and fathers of children at risk of ending up in foster care have adequate income. This program mitigates the stress of economic hardship on the family, which is often a precursor to abuse and neglect of the kids.

- **A CEO** of a large company champions a wellness plan that focuses on financial, emotional, and interpersonal Health. The CEO has witnessed that when those upstream wellness factors are out of balance her employees tend to need help with downstream issues like depression, substance abuse, stress, and anxiety.

- **A group of dentists** who regularly volunteer at free dental clinics in Kansas band together to lobby the legislature to increase Medicaid reimbursement rates for dental visits. This change will lead to more dentists accepting Medicaid and working with patients in poverty.

- **Harvesters, a food bank based in Kansas City,** provides food to food pantries across twenty-seven counties in Kansas and Missouri. They also launched several initiatives recently to influence policy that would keep people from becoming hungry in the first place.

Here are two examples of how KHF is bringing this mindset to life:

- **Change public policy.** KHF invests millions each year in policy work, which tends to be upstream because it pushes and pulls the levers that organize society. We promote policies that allow society to be organized in a way that makes Health the likely default rather than the exception.

- **Create leadership in Kansas.** It takes leadership to create change, which is why KHF continues to invest millions each year into the Kansas Leadership Center. The quantity and quality of leadership in Kansas communities is an upstream determinant of community Health.

Three Ways to Help Yourself and Others Work and Think More Upstream

1. **Talk about it.** When your company, church, or organization is thinking up a new initiative to help others, simply ask the question, "Is this downstream or upstream?" Simply spurring the conversation is helpful. Or go even further like the Kansas Health Institute did. They created a podcast called *Health on the Plains* that examines what's working upstream in rural communities.

2. **Balance your charitable contributions.** Keep contributing to charities doing downstream work but increase the percentage of your philanthropic contributions to organizations doing upstream work. Visit kansashealth.org/leadinghealth to see a list of the Kansas Health Foundation's current upstream partners.

3. **Analyze your downstream vs. upstream efforts.** The 30,000 are frequently a part of community and civic initiatives. For some of you, it's literally your full-time job. Look at your calendar for the last seven days and count the percent of your time spent on downstream versus upstream work. Share your results with others and ask them to do the same. Then challenge each other to increase the percentage of upstream efforts.

Why Charity Doesn't Change Things

Charity doesn't change things because it's not designed to change things. Here's an analogy: Ibuprofen treats the headache but not the reason you have the headache in the first place (i.e., stress, a lack of sleep, neurological disease, etc.). Charity treats the problem of homelessness, crime, etc., but not the reason people are homeless or crime is committed.

We need more upstream efforts to close The Health Gap. Upstream actions that might help include increasing public health funding per capita, improving fourth grade reading proficiency, ensuring broadband access to all communities, offering renewable energy alternatives, promoting policy efforts that create a more inclusive economy, and so on. To see progress in these and other upstream efforts we need the 30,000 to hold an upstream mindset that leads to upstream work.

CHAPTER 13

Mindset #2:
Work Systemically

To close The Health Gap, we need more of the 30,000 to
hold a systemic mindset. There are countless books on
the idea of systems thinking and I won't rehash them here.
But the pertinent point is that when trying to improve
the Health of a state, and specifically when trying to close
The Health Gap, we need our efforts to have the most bang
for the buck. Rather than helping one person, could we
work differently and help one hundred for the same amount
of work? Instead of helping one hundred people, could
we work differently and help one thousand or ten thousand
for the same amount of work? We'll need to do just that
to give ourselves a chance at leading the nation in Health.

That's another reason why I love America's Health Rankings.
It forces us to think bigger. We won't solve the affordable
housing crisis by building two homes in Wichita, one in
Pittsburg, and four in Johnson County. The individuals living
in those new affordable homes will have their lives changed.
That's good! But it won't move the rankings. Here are
some examples of the differences in the type of mindsets
we need:

- **Secondhand smoke**

  Individual mindset: Convincing a parent to stop smoking so their children don't suffer the consequences of secondhand smoke is good.
  Systemic mindset: Passing legislation, like the clean indoor air laws from the early 2010s, is better.

- **Education reform**

  Individual mindset: Helping one child escape a failing school is good.
  Systemic mindset: Creating policy that helps ensure all schools are successful so every student can succeed is better.

- **Business hiring policies**

  Individual mindset: A large business creating an exception in their hiring policy so they can hire a convicted felon is good.
  Systemic mindset: That same business deciding to stop asking about past criminal convictions in job applications is better.

- **Food accessibility**

  Individual mindset: Delivering fresh fruits and vegetables to one family in a food desert is good.
  Systemic mindset: Changing economic development policy to make a grocery store economically viable in the food desert is better. Also, businesses innovating and scaling low-cost grocery delivery solutions is better too.

Let's juxtapose the systemic mindset with the upstream mindset from the last chapter. Take a look at the 2x2 graph. Many Kansas do-gooder efforts are in box one. They are focused on charity for individuals which are downstream interventions. When transformative work does happen in Kansas, it's usually in box two—downstream systemic interventions. These efforts are transforming lives. That's good! It's at such a small scale that neighborhood, community, or state-level change is unlikely.

Sometimes Kansans rally and we end up in box three, individual upstream interventions. Those efforts look like massive amounts of financial contributions after a natural disaster. Those are often inspiring and heartwarming efforts. But what we need to transform Health in Kansas are more systemic upstream intervention efforts in box four!

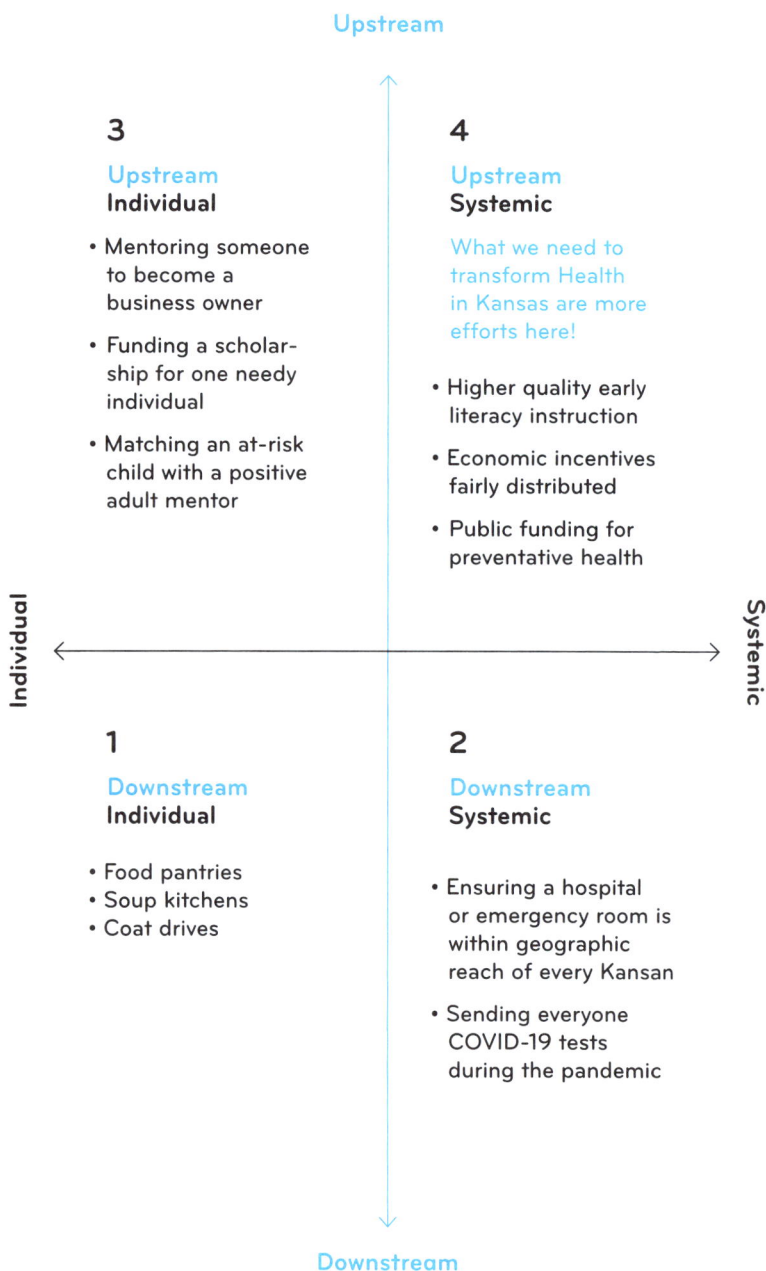

Upstream

3
Upstream
Individual

- Mentoring someone to become a business owner
- Funding a scholarship for one needy individual
- Matching an at-risk child with a positive adult mentor

4
Upstream
Systemic

What we need to transform Health in Kansas are more efforts here!

- Higher quality early literacy instruction
- Economic incentives fairly distributed
- Public funding for preventative health

Individual ←→ **Systemic**

1
Downstream
Individual

- Food pantries
- Soup kitchens
- Coat drives

2
Downstream
Systemic

- Ensuring a hospital or emergency room is within geographic reach of every Kansan
- Sending everyone COVID-19 tests during the pandemic

Downstream

- **Examples of downstream individual interventions (box one):** Food pantries. Soup kitchens. Coat drives.

- **Examples of downstream systemic interventions (box two):** Ensuring a hospital or emergency room is within geographic reach of every Kansan. Sending everyone COVID-19 tests during the pandemic.

- **Examples of upstream individual interventions (box three):** Mentoring someone to become a business owner. Funding a scholarship for one needy individual. Matching an at-risk child with a positive adult mentor.

- **Examples of upstream systemic interventions (box four):** Policy change that mandates higher quality early literacy instruction at every Kansas school. Economic incentives available to everyone and fairly distributed. Funding preventative public health initiatives.

All those efforts are good and worthy, but some (the upstream and systemic ones) are better than others at helping Kansas thrive. It's good to teach financial literacy to one young person living in an impoverished neighborhood (box one). But adding a financial literacy course requirement to the K-12 curriculum in all Kansas schools is better (box four). Buying a YMCA membership for one ALICE family, so they have a safe place to exercise, is good (box one). But cities adopting policies that require walkable neighborhoods (complete with sidewalks, pedestrian friendly intersections, and parks), making it possible to exercise for free outside is better (box four).

Three Ways to Help Yourself and Others Work and Think More Systemically

1. **Talk about it.** When your organization is thinking up a new initiative to help others, simply ask the question, "Is this a systemic or individual-by-individual approach?"

2. **Download the 2x2.** The 2x2 graph from this chapter is available at kansashealth.org/leadinghealth. List in each box the nonprofit and do-gooder efforts you are fond of and/or you contribute your time, energy, or money to personally and professionally. Ideally, a good mix of organizations emerge in all boxes. Simply updating the chart quarterly will help you become more conscious of the upstream versus downstream mindset.

3. **Don't get lost in the jargon.** I've heard too many people with too many degrees lecture me and others about "systems thinking". The diagrams and theories are dizzying. Keep it simple. Systemic work affects a lot of people. Individual work affects one or a few. Think of systemic work as a highly efficient way to bring about the change you desire. It's really that simple.

Here's one last example to help you understand the systemic mindset: My dad battled Parkinson's disease for eighteen years. I volunteer at Club Parkinson's, an exercise and support community for those battling the disease. My monthly contribution to Club Parkinson's makes membership fees more affordable. That's good but it's still an individual intervention in box one. A box four systemic effort related to Parkinson's might look like funding research to understand what's fueling the dramatic increase of Parkinson's (which is now the fastest growing brain disease in the world).

The 30,000 need to become better at recognizing, imagining, and valuing systemic approaches to creating Health. We simply don't have the resources to affect enough change with an individual-by-individual approach. Our challenge is to keep encouraging the good work that helps individual Kansans while using our positions and leadership to ensure there are enough complementary systemic approaches.

CHAPTER 14

Mindset #3:
Race and Racism Matters

Different races have different Health outcomes. The causes of these differential outcomes have been explored and researched numerous times by others. I'm not attempting to offer all that analysis here. You can visit kansashealth.org/leadinghealth to find a list of resources if you are interested in learning more about the connections between race and Health. To me, it's obvious that the way our society is organized leads to more Health for some and less Health for others. And those differences in Health are delineated, unfortunately, by race.

We all know that America doesn't have a shining record when it comes to fostering good discourse about race. But to close The Health Gap, Kansas must become a place that helps more and more people have useful and insightful discourse about race and racism. If we don't, I'm not sure how The Health Gap closes. Kansas needs the 30,000 to help create greater understanding about race and racism and their connection to Health.

The most hideous inequities are the results of racism—blatant racism and its more elusive cousin systemic racism. Have you been to what used to be the epicenter of Black Wall Street in Tulsa, Oklahoma? Three feelings emerged while I stood recently at the site of the 1922 Tulsa Race Massacre:

First, I was overwhelmed that it happened. I love America, but not this particular tragic part of our past, and all it represents. I was nauseous standing there over one hundred years later. Second, I was surprised to learn that the 1922 massacre didn't bring the end of Black Wall Street. The 1940s saw the neighborhood at its peak in terms of prosperity, opportunity, and energy. Third, I became acutely aware of systemic forces. There's not much of Black Wall Street left, just half a block. Interstate 244, built in the 1960s, cuts through the neighborhood. A massacre couldn't kill this vibrant center of Black wealth. But a massive highway project did. Maybe the engineers and highway planners were consciously conniving on how to hurt the Black families that lived there. Or maybe they just didn't even think about the generational impact on those families. There are sins of commission and sins of omission. The Tulsa Race Massacre was blatant, disgusting racism at its worst. Locating I-244 there is a perfect example of systemic racism.

The highway engineers, city planners, government representatives, and business officials who built an interstate system in Tulsa didn't engineer a horrific event like the Tulsa Race Massacre. But that doesn't mean the results haven't been horrific for the Health of Black families in Tulsa. Countless other examples of Health being impacted by racism or systemic racism exist.

To close The Health Gap, we must understand and address the implicit forces that perpetuate inequities. A first step is understanding that systemic racism is real. It's easy to spot explicit racism—slavery, redlining, denial of civil rights, violence, etc. But we all must learn to see systemic racism. That's hard because discerning systemic racism requires the ability to engage and discuss differences without fear, malice, or defensiveness from all parties. Those who believe they see systemic racism need the forum and space to share their experience. Those who have contrary thoughts about whether something is systemic racism also need that same opportunity. A culture that cancels dissent is no better than a culture that assumes our race issues are all in the past.

Remember the big picture. For the marginalized, the effect isn't much different whether the racism is explicit or systemic. Health outcomes suffer either way. At least you can see a racist mob coming.

The Kansas Health Foundation recently made our biggest commitment yet to racial equity. (See further along in this chapter for how I define "equity.") We committed $30,000,000 to thirty organizations on the front lines of promoting racial equity related to Health. Building the power and influence of organizations like these, that are in and of the communities facing the greatest Health disparities, is a prerequisite for more progress on issues related to Health, race, and racism.

What It Could Look Like for the 30,000 to Hold a Mindset That Race and Racism Matters for Health

- **Economic development organizations** would track the economic incentives used in all areas of a city and would spur conversation when/if less is invested in traditionally Black or Latino parts of town.

- **School districts** in cities would rebuild urban schools rather than moving them to greenspace on the fringes of the district, allowing urban kids (who are more often Black and Latino) to attend school close to home.

- **Government officials** would commission efforts to understand how racism of the past has led to systemic racism of the present.

- **Companies** would diversify supply chains and look for opportunities to help build wealth among Black and Brown businesses, neighborhoods, and families.

- **Banks** would lead efforts to help cities, economic development agencies, and developers understand the impact of the racist practice of redlining, which denied thousands of Black Kansan families the opportunity to build wealth through homeownership.

Three Ways to Help Yourself and Others Understand That Race and Racism Matters When It Comes to Health

1. **Help others understand the dominant perspectives on this topic.** I keep copies of three excellent books related to race and racism on my desk. I refer to the three of them often when in discussions with others. The three books are stand-ins for what I think are the dominant orientations to the topic in our country. I'm generalizing of course, but Ian Rowe's *Agency* reflects the political right's perspective. George Yancy's *Beyond Racial Division* reflects a more centrist perspective. Heather McGhee's *The Sum of Us* reflects the political left's perspective. All three are excellent and all three believe the outcomes certain populations are achieving are unacceptable. I talk about these books and give out copies often to help people understand there are different perspectives on the causes of the problems and how to solve them. But there is actually pretty good consensus across the political spectrum that there is, in fact, a problem.

2. **Create space for discourse.** We need more places—in public and private life—where Kansans can have good, high-quality discussions about race and racism. Those places are becoming hard to find. Use your authority to create those spaces. Leadership by the 30,000—by you—can help create that ability for communication between all Kansans. We need engagement that creates

integration not isolation, that leads to working together rather than apart, especially on the connections of race, racism, and Health.

3. **Define "equity" as "equality of opportunity," rather than "equality of outcomes".** I've noticed the latter leads to zero-sum thinking, the fear of a fixed pie that is going to be redistributed. I've noticed the former leads to a growth mindset and helps people avoid the knee jerk polarization that comes anytime someone attempts to redistribute wealth and resources.

Roland S. Martin, the prominent American journalist, gave a stirring keynote speech on Martin Luther King Jr. Day in 2023 in Wichita. To my recollection, the point of his magnificent speech, which I remember him making at the top of his lungs several times, was simple: "Show us the money!" I understood his purpose was to raise the heat on the well-meaning programs, training, and DEI-related activities, and force attention to focus on actual outcomes and specifically the economic outcomes of Black families. To close The Health Gap, we must elevate the economic opportunity for Black and Brown Kansans. We must eliminate the inequities that create Health disparities. We must ensure the same opportunity for Health exists no matter the race of Kansans.

CHAPTER 15

Mindset #4:
Create Collaboration

Encouraging collaboration is fine. Just about everyone does that. To close The Health Gap, you need to shift from "encouraging" to using your leadership and authority to "create" collaboration. Most people involved with Health in Kansas know we need more and better collaboration among the public, private, and nonprofit sectors to make more progress on Health. There has also been a surge of understanding that involving those with lived experience is critical for successful collaboration. Many in the 30,000 have been encouraging collaboration for decades. Kansas would literally become Healthier if there were more activities like:

- **Adjacent county health departments** creating more efficiencies through shared administration, freeing up more money for needed services.

- **Traditional economic development organizations** (which traditionally have healthy budgets) partnering with grassroots organizations (which usually have small budgets) to promote economic growth in communities facing the greatest disparities.

- **The fifty-plus organizations** focused on early literacy in Wichita combining efforts, streamlining services, and putting more money and resources into helping kids read rather than administering their organizations.

- **Private sector companies** engaging with strategic thought partners in the nonprofit and civic space to learn how their private sector feel-good fundraising galas can create the most actual impact on the ground.

- **Foundations** working together, combining their resources and efforts, to simplify things for grantees and to model the very type of collaboration they hope to see across Kansas.

On one hand, collaboration related to Health has been on the rise the last twenty years. There are shining examples of collaborative efforts leading to progress. Blue Cross Blue Shield of Kansas has invested heavily in its Pathways initiative, which provides financial resources and support to community Health coalitions. The results have been impressive, with countless policies changed to support Health in local government and within organizations or companies. Another fantastic example is the effort spearheaded by the Sunflower Foundation to create collaboration between behavioral health and primary care services. Dozens of primary care and family practice doctors' offices across Kansas are now co-located with behavioral health specialists. The result is better treatment and more integrated care for Kansans. On the other hand, we don't see highly productive collaboration very often. Shining examples are encouraging, but rare. My guess is that some of you are reading this and getting a bit defensive. You are thinking about other successful collaborations you've experienced. That's great! I could also list more positive examples. The point is they aren't the norm!

The norm is for organizations and initiatives to become more separate and to work more independently. It's human nature. People crave working on their own, with little influence or need to compromise, so they consciously and subconsciously keep creating new organizations, departments, committees, etc. All of this often leaves well-intended people unable to see opportunities for working together.

Three Examples of How KHF Is Bringing This Mindset to Life in Our Work

1. **Our network mobilization initiative** is designed to help our core partners work together each year on one of the fifty plus measures in America's Health Rankings. We are using our authority to create expectations for that collaboration and make resources available to help it happen.

2. **Other foundations and KHF** know we need to model what we hope to see from nonprofits across Kansas and so we are creating plans to demonstrate more collaboration.

3. **We regularly convene our grant partners** working on policy change. We have created an expectation that more progress is made when the partners plan, work, and evaluate their performances together.

And here's another example from one of our core partners, the Kansas Health Institute (KHI). They brought together Kansans from every corner of the state to create Age-Friendly Kansas, helping traditionally siloed sectors (e.g., health care, aging services, and public health) work together on an initiative to transform how the elderly are supported.

Here Are Five Approaches You Can Use to Make Collaboration More Successful and to Create More of It

1. **Anchor the collaboration.** The best examples of successful collaboration for Health in Kansas tend to revolve around a specific and bold objective. Examples include coalitions created in the 2000s focused on creating clean indoor air (think smoke free) throughout Kansas communities. The phenomenal and expansive recent effort to modernize the Kansas behavioral health system is another example. A mayor could create a task force charged with ending hunger in her city. A CEO could charge a cross-functional team with crafting new policies to increase wellness, measured by winning a "Healthiest Place to Work" award and increasing

employee satisfaction scores. Collaborating for the sake of collaboration doesn't usually yield results. Make it specific.

2. **Require collaboration.** That might sound harsh, but it's more common than you think. The legislature forces collaboration by requiring a conference committee (made up of legislators from both chambers) to create legislation most likely to pass. State law often requires an affirmative vote from a local school district, city, and county to utilize economic development tools. That forces those units of government to work together.

    Collaboration to advance Health could look like a county manager requiring public health and economic development officials to prepare a "Health impact assessment" for new developments. A foundation could require grant applicants to have at least two partners from different sectors as part of their application.

3. **Build support for collaboration.** Collaboration is hard, but it's much easier with people skilled at helping others work together and at bringing the right data and information to the table. Resource collaborative efforts with professional capacity like high-quality meeting facilitators and researchers.

4. **Share power with those with lived experience.** Listening to those with lived experience has become a norm, but sharing power with them? That's next level collaboration,

and it's sorely needed. KHI has learned that for collaboration to be transformational, you can't just hear from those with lived experience. Instead, use your authority to make them an essential part of the collaboration.

5. **Remember this simple formula.** One of my mentors, David Chrislip, taught me a simple formula for effective collaboration. If you bring the right people together (who aren't always your usual people), with good information, and do so in a healthy process, you'll get positive results every time.

   Right people + good information + healthy process = progress

   It's really that simple. And you can use your leadership and authority to make people tend to those three components.

Collaboration is hard because you lose some control when you collaborate. It implies working together and a joint agenda. No one thinks of themselves as someone who likes to be in a silo, but most of us end up working in silos. Why? Because we like the control that comes with the silo. Collaboration requires us to negotiate our desires alongside others' desires. We must find a way forward that gets us enough of what we want and helps others get enough of what they want. That's tricky, which is why effective collaboration is rare.

Collaboration feels slow but speeds things up. It seems complicated but simplifies things. It looks costly but saves money. Collaboration has those superpowers because, when done right, it helps people finally make progress on issues that organizations and communities have been wrestling with for years.

All of this speaks to why you and the 30,000 need a mindset of creating collaboration. Kansas needs you to create the conditions—the collaborative conditions—so we can make more progress closing The Health Gap and helping Kansas lead the nation in Health.

CHAPTER 16

Mindset #5:

Value Process and Structure

I'm going to try to explain something in this chapter that is quite nebulous. Please hang with me. I need to shine a light on one of the most important yet hidden skills needed for transformative, game-changing work: the ability to imagine the right process and structure to bring the change to life.

Those words—process and structure—are wonky. They might make you yawn. I'm grappling with an idea that I haven't seen articulated well elsewhere. But after participating and watching civic and organizational life in Kansas and beyond for over twenty-five years, I'm confident that "process and structure" are under-valued by those who want change— change like closing The Health Gap.

My former colleague and good friend Mike Matson first introduced those words—"process and structure"—to me. I was a young staffer for the governor. He was older than me and was the press secretary, which I thought had to be the coolest job in the office. I valued every minute I got to spend with him. He later guided communication efforts at the Kansas Leadership Center. I had the following experience countless times:

Ed describes a nutty idea or vision.

Mike asks what kind of process and structure is needed to bring it to life.

Ed looks at Mike dumbfounded. "Process and structure? What do you mean?"

Eventually, I got it. Mike knew intuitively what took me several years to learn and what I'm trying to share in this chapter. The best visions in the world are worthless without someone inventing the process and structure to bring them to life. I'm going to share two examples from my own experience and three examples from others to bring this idea to life.

From the beginning, the people at the Kansas Leadership Center knew they wanted to work at a scale never seen in traditional leadership development programs. The vision was just a vision until Thomas Stanley and Shaun Rojas invented the process and structure that became Leadership Transformation Grants, a mechanism that would help the center reach thousands of additional Kansans each year.

At the Kansas Health Foundation, we knew our partners working on policy could have more impact working together. That vision started to come to fruition when Drew Wilburne and Jazmine Rogers invented the necessary process and structures to make it happen. They started designating certain partners as Policy Partners, providing a joint training opportunity for them called KHF Summer School, co-creating a logic model that described the vision, holding regular meetings where the CEOs of those organizations could meet, and much more.

In the mid-1800s Americans started playing lots of baseball. The sport was becoming a favorite of kids and adults all over our young country. And there were likely visionaries who could see the sport sweeping the land and becoming the national pastime. But the real visionaries were the people who looked at the situation and thought, "For this to work, we are going to need a league with teams." And later another visionary thought, "What we should do is combine those leagues into one 'Major League'. And there should be a host of feeder teams that develop players and send the best ones to the major teams." I've oversimplified, of course, but you get the idea. Someone had to invent the process and structure to help our country go from a place that loves baseball to baseball becoming the national pastime.

In the 1990s there was a growing recognition that as the population of rural Kansas continued to decline, the wealth that was built there would gradually leave those counties. The children of wealthy families were less likely to remain in rural towns. So over time, generational wealth would be inherited by family members with less and less connection to rural Kansas. The result would be less community philanthropy available to support all sorts of important causes.

To counter this, a few key thinkers at the Kansas Health Foundation had a vision to dramatically increase community philanthropy across Kansas. They invented a process and structure (matching grants, training, creation of a statewide association of community foundations, and more) that led to the creation of dozens of community foundations across Kansas. Today the result is hundreds of millions of philanthropic dollars benefiting Kansans.

In 2004 bright minds in the Kansas Legislature knew that spurring entrepreneurship was key to our state's future. That knowledge wasn't revolutionary. A lot of people agreed. But what had been missing was an effective process and structure to spread entrepreneurship at scale. Two legislators, Representative Kenny Wilk and Senator Nick Jordan, guided the way to create Network Kansas. Steve Radley was hired to lead the effort. Kenny, Nick, and Steve all could dream big dreams, but they also had a knack for creating the process and structure needed to make the dreams happen. Network Kansas today is one of the most innovative and successful entrepreneurship endeavors I've seen in Kansas or beyond. The reason is the process and structure components. The funding rests on a tax credit business model (which is brilliant for reasons I don't have the space to explain here). They created "E-Communities" across the state and gave the decision-making ability, about which entrepreneurs to fund, to those local teams. An annual event networks those teams with each other and other entrepreneurial support organizations. They have multiple funds they use to invest, with debt or equity, into businesses owned by Kansas entrepreneurs.

Here are some other quick examples:

- **Long ago there was a vision to create economic incentives for new development in cities.** Some people had to invent the process and structure we now call "tax increment financing districts."

- **Long ago there was a vision for a healthier state.** Some people had to invent the process and structure of a County Board of Health, county health officers, and the state agency we call the Kansas Department of Health and Environment.

- **Long ago there was a vision for how businesses working together could prosper more.** Some people had to invent the process and structure we now know as chambers of commerce.

- **Long ago there was a vision for using universities to elevate the conditions of the working people of the United States.** Some people had to invent the process and structure we now know as land-grant universities like Kansas State University.

What Process and Structure Must Be Invented

To lead the nation in Health and to close The Health Gap, new processes and structures might look like this:

- **Process and structure** to make regional collaboration more likely on all the aspects that make up Health.

- **Process and structure** to make it so every student in communities facing the greatest disparities get connected to high quality culturally competent mentors.

- **Process and structure** to make it likely that the private sector, government sector, and nonprofit sector are working in sync at the state, regional, county, city, and neighborhood level.

- **Process and structure** to make public engagement at government meetings more productive. (Think about it. The open mic public comment period is a type of process and structure. Someone had to invent that idea. Given that it's most often just political theater today, a new process and structure to ensure public engagement and input is warranted.)

Four Ways to Help Increase the Value of Process and Structure

1. **Ask questions about it.** Channel my friend Mike Matson. "What kind of process and structure is needed for that objective or vision to become reality?"

2. **Name and question the process and structure you are already utilizing.** See the things you are required to do each week (i.e., attend this meeting, submit that report, update this organization, conduct this process, finalize that contract, etc.) as parts of the existing process and structure you operate within.

3. **Don't take the "how" for granted.** When it comes to visions and strategic initiatives, don't take the "how" for granted. So often the 30,000 are focused on the "why" or the "what." That's fine, that's the big strategic stuff. But the process and structure decisions will make or break your big strategic visions.

4. **See process and structure as a creative, entrepreneurial task.** Treat the development of process and structure as a creative act, rather than an administrative one. To close The Health Gap and help Kansas lead the nation in Health we'll need to invent so many new ways of working together. That means we'll need creators and inventors in our midst.

For most game-changing efforts, we need to be able to imagine two distinct things: a vision and the process and structure to bring that vision to life. The former is hard. The latter is harder. Lots of people had visions about baseball becoming ubiquitous in America, philanthropy flourishing in rural communities, or entrepreneurship scaling across Kansas. But only a few people knew the real challenge was creating the process and structure to bring each of those visions to fruition. Use your leadership to help others value the process and structure that will be needed to close The Health Gap in our state, but also in your part of it.

CHAPTER 17

Mindset #6:
Policy Over Politics

To close The Health Gap and to help Kansas lead the nation in Health, we'll need to focus on policy more and politics less. As a former legislator and a former candidate for governor, I appreciate politics as much as anyone. But I also see how our society has slowly sorted into two meta factions: one left, one right. Progress on our toughest issues almost always requires engagement across differences. Closing The Health Gap is no exception.

A challenge for improving Health in Kansas is to discern the line between policy advocacy and political advocacy. Policy advocacy is the work of mobilizing elected officials to support or oppose specific legislation. Political advocacy is the work of changing the make-up of those elected officials. Both have their place. But blending them, which happens often these days, can make progress on policy change hard. Why? Because it's hard to have policy discussions with elected officials who perceive you just spent an entire campaign trying to defeat them.

I'm not naïve to the work of politics. I understand it has its place. But for Kansas to close The Health Gap and lead the nation in Health, the 30,000 need to model "next level" discourse that elevates policy over politics. Most policy work is upstream. That's why it's so important for Health. But it's a mistake to assume that only one party or faction has all the right ideas to help Kansas lead the nation in Health. There are progressive and conservative policy ideas that are needed. We'll need a mixture of both to climb to number one.

My experience is that transformative policy change requires three distinct groups of people and organizations: advocates, activists, and bridgers.

- **Advocates** speak their mind.

- **Activists** mobilize advocates and create more of them.

- **Bridgers** work to find connecting interests among advocates and activists.

All three types are needed.

There's been a surge of advocates and activists in recent years. I assume two factors are driving that increase: ease of engagement via technology and reaction to the extremism of the left and right. At the same time, it seems there are fewer bridgers today than there have ever been. There aren't many rewards for being a bridger. You get figuratively beat up from both sides.

The Kansas Health Foundation has made a conscious choice that while we fund advocates and even some activists, our best role in policy change is to be a bridger. We don't think everyone should be a bridger, but we do believe bridgers are in short supply.

What It Would Look Like if More of the 30,000 Held a Policy Over Politics Mindset

- **Groups:** More policy agendas of chambers of commerce, nonprofits, and others would have policies on their wish list that are acceptable to the political left, center, and right.

- **Voting:** There would be a surge of voter registration efforts co-created and executed by organizations with different political leanings.

- **Compromise:** More policy compromise would occur because policy advocates and activists would expect it and therefore not punish elected officials for it.

Suggestions to Help You Hold a Policy Over Politics Mindset

1. **Make a conscious choice about whether you are a policy advocate, activist, or bridger?** All three are needed, but it should be a conscious choice. And notice I used "policy" as the modifier not "political."

2. **Take a partisan inventory of "your people."** If you are surrounded only by people on the right or left, make a conscious effort to diversify your circle.

3. **Let data do the work.** Data walks are a new way of starting engagement on important policy questions. Pioneered in Kansas by the Kansas Health Institute and the Legacy Community Foundation in Cowley County, a data walk brings diverse people together not to debate policies, but to make sense out of troubling data about Health in their community. By making the data the focus, rather than preferred strategies of one political faction or another, participants engage better and a consensus forms to resolve the underlying situation.

4. **Find and use objective sources for information.** The Kansas Health Institute can create those data walks because they are a trusted source of objective information for people across the political spectrum. Find and use credible organizations like KHI that exist to provide objective information and not to advance a particular position.

5. **Trust voters.** There is a direct connection between voter participation and Health. America's Health Rankings agrees. Voter participation is one of the measures that makes up the overall Health rankings. Increasing voter participation contributes to the best possible policy decisions over time and is a proxy for personal and community agency. But too many efforts designed to

increase voter participation seem less about increasing
agency and more like blatant campaigns to elect certain
types of politicians—either progressive or conservative,
depending on the entity doing the voter engagement
work. Honor the power and agency of each voter to
determine for themselves what issues and which candi-
dates deserve their support.

Enough of the 30,000 having a policy over politics mindset
will foster unity not division and consensus not polarization.
Most of all, it will foster problem-solving.

The great Kansas journalist William Allen White, who
became a dominant force in Republican affairs in Kansas
and America in the early 1900s, knew this was important.
White once wrote a letter to Charles Gleed, of the *Kansas
City Journal*, "It takes all kinds of people to make a world
and I am willing to admit that the conservative brake on the
progressive wheel is a good thing."

Policy work is often the ultimate upstream work for Health.
The more American politics engulfs the 30,000, the less
likely we'll have the discourse and consensus we need for
necessary policy change. And the less that happens, the less
chance there is to close The Health Gap. The ALICE families
and others experiencing the greatest Health disparities
need you to model a policy over politics mindset. Doing
so will create more progress on Health.

CHAPTER 18

Mindset #7:
Embrace Bold Vision

Don't hate me for saying this, but there aren't many examples of Kansas organizations shooting for world-class excellence. There are some, of course. The Kansas Jayhawks start every basketball season with the goal of winning a national championship. K-State recently adopted a new strategic plan to become the model land-grant university for the 21st century. The Wichita YMCA system is likely the best in the world, and those running it strive to continue that excellence. The University of Kansas Hospital System strives to provide the highest level of patient care in the country. The Kansas Leadership Center has a vision to be the center of excellence for leadership development. Exploration Place in Wichita strives to offer the best science museum experience in the world. The Kansas State Department of Education's strategic plan—Kansas Can—casts a vision for Kansas to lead the world in the success of each student.

These examples are inspiring, but they are far from the norm. The Kansas "aw shucks" spirit often creates an "average and damn proud of it" mindset. The deep listening referred to earlier identified that a lack of bold aspirations was getting in the way of progress. Kansans intuitively understand that bold visions create healthy pressure to elevate our efforts and reach better outcomes. Average or ambiguous visions lower pressure. Without bolder visions, Kansas will likely remain middle of the road, or worse, when it comes to Health.

The boldness of your vision corresponds to the level of pressure on your people. Consider these two batches of vision statements. The first batch turns up the heat. The second batch conveys things that are important but don't pack the same punch as the first.

Examples of bold vision statements:

- **A principal** casts a vision for the highest test scores in the district.

- **A mayor** casts a vision to create more new units of affordable housing than any other community in the state.

- **A group** of Rotary Club presidents come together to cast a vision for Kansas to lead the nation in the number of mental health professionals per capita. (By the way, this is in the works! Kansas Rotarians are exploring a game-changing initiative for mental health in Kansas, just like the Rotarian worldwide efforts to combat polio.)

And here are some fine statements that lack bold vision:

- **A school's mission** is to provide a quality learning experience for every student in every classroom, every day.

- **A nonprofit's primary goal** is to advance education, financial stability, and health for those living in its six-county region.

- **The vision for a state advocacy organization** is that all Kansans reach their full potential.

The bold visions listed first are specific and convey greatness. The second set of statements are fine, but are also obvious or even perfunctory. We need more of the former and less of the latter if we are going to close The Health Gap and help Kansas lead the nation in Health. Bold visions create pressure on ourselves. That's the point and that's why Kansans told us bolder visions were needed. We need healthy pressure to do our best. Without enough of that pressure we slowly, and without much notice, slid from being one of the Healthiest states to below average.

Work underway at the Wichita Fire Department is modeling this bold vision mindset. What started as an effort to help firefighters access cancer screening each year has turned into a visionary objective to create a model culture of wellness in the fire department. I've been loosely connected to this work. From the very beginning, everyone knew the work was important, but as the vision became bigger and bolder the energy and enthusiasm from all involved kept increasing. Now the energy is captivating. Something transformative is underway that goes so much further than the original project. That's what bold visions do. They unleash optimism, enthusiasm, and commitment you don't get otherwise. We need those three things if we are going to close The Health Gap.

Here Are Two Examples of How KHF Is Trying to Bring This Mindset to Life

1. **In our purpose.** Our three-part purpose statement heaps tons of bold, healthy pressure on us. Part One is to help Kansas lead the nation in Health. Part Two is to eliminate the inequities that create health disparities. Part Three is to become the model for philanthropic impact.

2. **In our investing.** Our board recently approved $58 million from our endowment to be used for impact investing. This is the process of investing a portion of our endowment in Kansas businesses that create social impact and generate financial return. We carefully and consciously set two goals for that $58 million. First, to make money while doing good. Second, to catalyze other foundations to use a portion of their endowments for impact investing as well. Encouraging other foundations will likely unleash hundreds of millions of additional dollars for Health-related efforts in Kansas. The boldness of the second goal pushes us to think and act much differently than if we just had the first goal.

What's the boldest version of your aspirations? You and the 30,000 have more ability to dial up the boldness in the mission, vision, and purpose statements of organizations across Kansas. Look at those statements for your organization and other organizations you are involved with. On a scale of one to ten, how bold are they? How could you take it up a notch?

There is a downside to casting bolder visions. You could be setting yourself up for disappointment. Afterall, Coach Bill Self doesn't guide the Jayhawks to a championship every year. Keep in mind the quote from Mark Twain, "Aim above the mark to hit the mark." He was using a bow and arrow metaphor to make a point about human striving. We might not hit what we aim for, but we'll hit higher than we would have otherwise.

And here's one last thought especially for my friends worried about the cost of big and bold visions. (I'm looking at you, my nonprofit and government friends!) My experience is that big, bold, logical ideas get funded. Yes, bold ideas often cost more to bring to fruition. But that boldness is also what attracts energy and resources.

CHAPTER 19

Mindset #8:
Leverage Economic Forces

One of the best things I've read about creating social change is the book *Forces for Good* by Leslie Crutchfield and Heather McLeod Grant. The authors researched twelve nonprofits they deemed to be high-impact organizations, including Habitat for Humanity, The Heritage Foundation, America's Second Harvest, and National Council of La Raza. One of the practices all these high-impact nonprofits had in common was their ability to "make markets work," meaning they found ways to unleash market and economic forces to help them advance their social cause.

The Kansas gross domestic product (GDP) in 2023 was about $220 billion dollars. GDP is a good indicator of overall economic activity. I think of that $220 billion as a system of interests, organizations, priorities, and values. When taken all together, that system is producing all the results we are experiencing in Kansas. Here's a meta way of thinking about it: That GDP is giving us all our current Health outcomes. The Kansas Health Foundation is trying to intervene in that $220 billion system with about $25 to $30 million per year. That's not even a drop in a bucket.

It's a drop in the ocean! The point is that if we want to close The Health Gap and help Kansas lead the nation in Health, we'll need a lot more of us to have a "leverage economic forces" mindset.

We need to look for opportunities to connect Health efforts to the private sector for two reasons. First, because that's where most Kansans spend most of their time. If employers make their organizations more conducive for Health, Kansas will become Healthier. The second reason we need to connect Health to the private sector is because there isn't enough money flowing from or to Health-specific organizations to get the job done. What I'm getting at here is that to lead the nation in Health, we'll need to get more of that $220 billion to do work for the Health of Kansas.

Leveraging economic forces looks like:

- **Impact investing,** which I described earlier. Investing $58 million from the Kansas Health Foundation endowment in global markets is fine. But investing $58 million in Kansas—for profit and for social change—is a smart move. We dream of an impact-investing ecosystem fueling hundreds of millions of additional investments into Health-oriented efforts in Kansas. That's not far-fetched. There are billions held in endowments in Kansas. That money is invested in real estate in Boston, tech companies in Silicon Valley, and countless other places. Imagine if 5% of that was redirected to investments in Kansas. That would be millions of dollars being put to work to foster Health via the private sector. And because those aren't grant dollars, they get reinvested repeatedly. Which means they are multiplying themselves and creating an ecosystem of private capital influencing Health.

- **Nonprofits adopting more social enterprise business models.** A nonprofit with this type of business model is a mission-oriented organization trying to do good and create social change, but they rest on a business model that feels more like a for-profit company. Examples in Kansas include Envision, Goodwill Industries, Kansas Leadership Center, and Raise My Head Foundation. These organizations sell their products or services to fuel their charitable and social missions. Not every nonprofit is suitable for the social enterprise business model. But those that can go this direction experience a pace of continual improvement that far outpaces the typical charitable organization. They also become less reliant on traditional charitable giving and grant writing, freeing up more resources for nonprofits that must rely on those approaches for funding.

- **Helping private companies focus on employee well-being and the company's bottom line.** Employers have a lot of influence over employees and, therefore, are smart leverage points. For years the Kansas Health Foundation worked with several hundred Kansas companies to help them create cultures of wellness. It was a win for the companies because it led to reduced health care costs and more engaged employees. It was a win for Health because it created more preventative measures and created new champions for Health promotion.

- **Scaling efforts to create economic leverage and efficiencies.** Steve Feilmeier, retired CFO of Koch Industries, is modeling the way on this. He created a multi-million dollar investment fund that is loaning money to culturally competent affordable housing developers. These developers are small businesses whose owners live in the very neighborhoods they are trying to serve and save. Steve's fund loans money at steep discounts to these developers, allowing them to build more houses with less money. It also uses Steve's business acumen, relationships, and his fund's credibility to streamline the supply chain for these developers. Allowing the developers to get access to materials and labor at significantly lower costs.

- **Making it easier for businesses to engage in Health.** The Kansas Health Foundation recently gave a $290,000 grant to Kanbe's Markets, an innovative nonprofit helping to solve the food desert problem in Kansas City. They partner with independent corner stores who usually sell highly processed food high in fat and sugar, along with tobacco and alcohol. Because of Kanbe's Markets, the corner stores end up selling fresh fruits and vegetables, but Kanbe's Markets assumes the responsibility and financial risk that comes with sourcing and stocking the products. It's a win-win model that helps the businesses do well financially and do good for the neighborhood at the same time.

Three Suggestions to Help You Hold a Leverage Economic Forces Mindset

1. **Ask about it.** When working on Health-related initiatives, the 30,000 should constantly ask questions like: "Where's the private sector in this? How could it be leveraged?"

2. **Create coalitions that involve the private sector.** Community coalitions working on Health are plentiful across Kansas. But most of them are made up of people almost entirely from the nonprofit and government sectors.

3. **Link charitable and philanthropic efforts to market forces.** For example, KHF, Stand Together Foundation, and several area banks in Wichita all partnered to develop an alternative to payday lending. The solutions include micro loans and matching savings, which serve as a bridge to mainstream banking for participants. Low-income Wichitans get financial help. Banks get customers. And Stand Together Foundation and KHF get the satisfaction of knowing our philanthropic resources are creating self-sufficiency, not dependency.

I know there are examples of the private sector, or private sector people, messing up Health. I'm not excusing that. I also understand that having a leverage economic forces mindset isn't a silver bullet that will solve all our problems.

It's just one of the mindsets we need more of if we are going to close The Health Gap.

Here's a final example, about Club Parkinson's again, which I mentioned earlier. The organization is phenomenal. The outcomes for the participants are almost miraculous. A recent study showed that over 80% of members stabilized or improved their symptoms. Now comes the connection to leveraging economic forces. Club Parkinson's is a non-profit based in Wichita, Kansas. With its current model, it can't even begin to reach all current or future Kansans with Parkinson's. But, Wichita is home to some of the most creative and successful franchise businesses in America, like Pizza Hut and White Castle. If my fellow Club Parkinson's volunteers and I keep thinking like a traditional nonprofit, we'll do good things, but we won't come close to scaling to fit the need. On the other hand, if we adopt a leverage economic forces mindset, Club Parkinson's might become the latest example of an amazing franchise brand created and scaled from Wichita.

CHAPTER 20

Mindset #9:
Make Metrics Matter

When it comes to creating a culture of learning and adaptation, the private sector has a key advantage over the nonprofit and government sectors. In the private sector, there is an obvious metric that motivates and propels people to improve: the bottom line. Other metrics are important, of course, but that one metric packs a punch and does so much work for private sector companies. By "work" I mean that the very existence of the metric spurs behavior changes in the company. If it's negative or not as positive as it used to be, everyone starts thinking and acting differently. If it stays negative, the company goes out of business. Learning and adaptation happens faster in the private sector because of this metric.

No such obvious metric exists in the nonprofit and government sectors. But metrics that pack a similar punch need to be identified or created if our organizations, coalitions, and movements working on Health are to succeed. And that will require you and enough of the 30,000 to hold a make metrics matter mindset.

You already know that I believe that America's Health Rankings are a useful and powerful metric. We've been able to ignite conversation and work across Kansas by simply using two data points from that existing data source. The first data point: We are 29th in Health. The second data point: We used to be 8th. A story was born with those two data points. And stories create action.

The point of measuring something is to create pressure to do something. In baseball we measure batting average, and sure enough hitters strive for a higher batting average. In football we measure total yards, and sure enough offenses strive to rack up as many yards as possible. Again, in the private sector we measure the bottom line, and sure enough companies strive to make a profit. What gets measured gets done.

A metric is useful if it propels action. If not, what's the point?

There's an epidemic in the nonprofit and government sectors of either having way too many metrics or no metrics at all. Too many metrics means no one knows what's important. It happens all the time. I remember early evaluation reports at the Kansas Leadership Center where we had a meandering conversation looking over our thirty-seven data points (none of which had more priority than others) from every program. A somewhat interesting conversation would ensue and then little would change. Nothing was packing a punch. We knew metrics were important, but we didn't yet hold a make metrics matter mindset. That situation is common. Technology today makes the "too many metrics" situation more likely because it's so easy to collect and share data. But just because you can collect the data doesn't mean it's useful.

The "no metric" situation is probably more prevalent. It can be hard to measure the impact of social and civic initiatives. That often leads to the creation of case studies or stories to convey impact. That's fine. And I understand the value of qualitative research. But often we just have anecdotes. Occasionally we get qualitative research, but it rarely packs a punch. It rarely propels the real-time learning and adaptation needed for transformative progress on issues connected to Health.

Sometimes holding a metric mindset means you need to invent that metric. Those thirty-seven data points at the Kansas Leadership Center? We scrapped them eventually and replaced them with one core metric that drove quality improvement for years. We called it the 80/80. One month after every program we asked our participants to respond to this statement: My KLC experience is helping me make progress on my leadership challenges. They could select one of multiple choices from strongly disagree to strongly agree. Our goal was to have an 80% response rate overall. And to have 80% of those responses be "strongly agree" or "agree."

Once we had the 80/80, we had a metric that packed a punch. We knew we had work to do if a score came back 43/59. We knew we could celebrate if it came back 93/98. Those earlier thirty-seven data points never packed that punch. They didn't propel our learning and improvement.

Years ago the University of Kansas Hospital started survey-ing every patient in the hospital every day. The question: On a one to five scale, how satisfied are you with your care today? Every day that data was collected and shared with every nurse, doctor, administrator, etc. The score could be broken down by floor and specialty. Every day they had a metric that packed a punch and helped them improve.

Community Solutions, a national group working to end homelessness, created a metric called "functional zero". A community hits functional zero when the number of people becoming homeless is below the number of people the community can shelter and assist into long-term housing. It's a brilliant example of inventing a metric to help gauge and drive performance.

To close The Health Gap we'll need more of the 30,000 using their leadership to help organizations and initiatives discover their own powerful metrics.

What Powerful Metrics Could Look Like

- **A school district superintendent** wants to propel improvement in the district, and knows to do so he needs a metric that is simple to understand, provocative, and collected frequently. He works with his team to invent a quarterly survey of all parents which asks: On a scale of one to five, how satisfied are you with the education of your student(s)? The first survey results gave a baseline response of 3.2. Now the superintendent can help principals create goals for the coming quarters for their individual schools and the overall school district.

- **The CEO** of an economic development organization realizes her metropolitan area can't prosper if there is a huge percentage of the population in poverty. She leads her staff and board of directors to adopt the percentage of population in poverty as a key metric used to gauge her organization's success.

Three Suggestions to Help You Hold a Make Metrics Matter Mindset

1. **Know the difference between evaluation, research, and key performance indicators.** Evaluation is about evaluating what happened. Research is about discovering new things. Key performance indicators, and goals associated with them, drive improvement and change.

2. **Invest more energy in key performance indicators.** Keep doing evaluation and research but find a metric or metrics (key performance indicators) that pack a punch. Find your version of the profit and loss statement of a private company, the satisfaction metric of the University of Kansas Hospital, or functional zero from Community Solutions.

3. **Invent a metric that works, if needed.** And remember, by "works" I mean a metric that, because it is tracked and discussed, propels people to do or consider things they wouldn't otherwise.

Those in authority (the 30,000 in Kansas community and civic life) need to provide direction if progress is to be made on adaptive challenges. As we've previously discussed and will discuss again in the next chapter, the 30,000 and you can't literally do all the work necessary to improve all the organizations, programs, and initiatives needed to improve Health in Kansas. But the work can't happen to the degree it needs to happen without you doing your share. What is your share? Part of it looks like making metrics matter.

Adaptive change is hard. But what you need to do to propel that change isn't always that hard to figure out. Use your leadership to align organizations and initiatives around powerful metrics that fuel performance. Pick the right metric or metrics, communicate about it all the time, and watch your system respond. Trust the process. Do your part and let others do theirs.

CHAPTER 21

Ten Things to Do Now

I've included lots of suggestions throughout this book, especially in each of the mindset chapters of Part Three. And I understand you already have a lot on your plate. I hope this book spurs big thoughts for you about your place in the overall Health journey of Kansas. I also want to make it easy for you to know how or where to start that journey. So, here are ten very specific actions you can take right now. In fact, please do one of these ten things literally right now. Read the ten. Pick one. Do it. And with that one action you'll already be doing more for Health in Kansas.

These ten things are not revolutionary. But that's kind of the point of this list. Bigger suggestions were nestled throughout the preceding pages. Do some of those things too. But these ten are straightforward, tactical actions. They are small things but represent big directions. You are already a busy person. I know it's hard to add things to your plate. Doing one of these ten actions is like a person trying to get back into shape. Their first trip to the gym doesn't make that person fit. But they can't become more fit without it.

Imagine if each of the 30,000 did one of these ten actions. Would we jump from 29th to first? Of course not, but there would be new, tangible momentum in that direction. Read the ten. Pick one. Do it. (My guess is it will lead to you picking a second item to help advance Health. Then a third. And so on.)

1. **Register for HealthRise.** Held for the first time in 2024, HealthRise is our annual event meant to anchor our journey to help Kansas lead the nation in Health. The purpose is to gather those who care about the journey, to celebrate our successes, to see the gaps that still exist, and to cast a vision for what needs to be done next. A vision for us as individuals and as a collective group of Kansans striving to help Kansas lead the nation in Health. Visit kansashealth.org/leadinghealth to find out how to join us at our next gathering.

2. **Apply for a Kansas Health Foundation Innovation Grant.** Ideas about ways to improve the Health of your organization, neighborhood, community, or region likely emerged in your mind while reading this book. Many of those ideas need financial resources to come to fruition. That's why we created the Kansas Innovation Fund. Apply for a grant now to fund that idea that's on your mind. The application is short, and we will get back to you quickly. The purpose of the fund is to spur experimentation and innovation. Visit kansashealth.org/opportunities/kansas-innovation-fund/ to apply.

3. **Share the Kansas snapshot from America's Health Rankings with your key people.** Rankings are provocative and catalyze conversation. Start one with key people in your organization. Visit kansashealth.org/leadinghealth and share the Kansas rankings within your executive team, entire organization, etc. Here's the message I suggest you use when you share: *Friends, there's an effort to make Kansas the Healthiest state in the nation. We're 29th. We used to be 8th. Look at this report and let me know your thoughts on what we could do to help within our organization, our community, and Kansas.*

4. **Share the Kansas snapshot with your elected officials.** Elected officials make up some of the 30,000. By now you know they play a key role in all things related to Health. Visit kansashealth.org/leadinghealth for a simple way to send a message to your elected officials at the local, state, and federal levels about the importance of Kansas climbing the rankings. (Remember, there are progressive and conservative ways to climb the rankings!)

5. **Join our crowdsourcing efforts.** Each year we engage Kansans to help crowdsource ideas on how to make game-changing, transformative progress on one of the measures that make up the health rankings. Visit kansashealth.org/leadinghealth to share a quick thought about the current crowdsourcing topic. Better yet, share the crowdsource link with those in your organization. Encourage or even incentivize their participation. Become part of the wisdom of the crowd.

6. **Use the Health Impact Checklist.** Created by the Kansas Health Institute, this tool has been tested in communities across Kansas and beyond, enabling officials to diagnose the potential health outcomes of their decisions. The tool helps decision-makers in city, county, and state governments recognize that decisions—whether in transportation, education, housing, or economic development—have profound health impacts. Find a link to the checklist at kansashealth.org/leadinghealth.

7. **Support your local Health coalition.** Visit kansashealth.org/leadinghealth to find a link to the contact information for the Health coalition(s) in your community. I recommend keeping it simple. Just send this message to the key contact listed: *I'm interested in learning more about how I can support your coalition. Please reach out to me at (your email or phone number inserted here).*

8. **Help us celebrate success and progress.** We need examples of Kansans doing what's needed to close The Health Gap and help Kansas lead the nation in Health. Visit kansashealth.org/leadinghealth to nominate a Kansan or Kansas organization that embodies one or more of the ideas shared in this book. We want to know their story and do our part to share it.

9. **Let me know your Health idea.** Email me at eomalley@khf.org. Seriously, that's my actual email. Let's start a conversation. Tell me how you think you can improve Health or how we could improve it together.

10. Get this book in the hands of other key Kansans.
Visit kansashealth.org/leadinghealth and give us
the name of one or more Kansans you know who should
read this book. We'll take it from there and send them
a copy. We will also make sure they know the idea came
from you.

Those are the ten. Pick one. Do it now. You'll feel good.
There will literally be more momentum in Kansas for Health
than there was before. Every small action matters. And did
you notice that each of those ten ideas, as well as the bigger
suggestions I offered throughout the book, require you to
engage with others?

Progress on Health in Kansas requires people to be mobilized who you can't force to be mobilized. Progress requires
financial resources to be redirected that you can't force to
be redirected. Progress requires values to be elevated that
you can't force to be elevated. You can't force any of it.
To lead the nation in Health, your leadership, whether you
are the governor, the vice-chancellor of the University
of Kansas Medical School, the CEO of a massive hospital
system, or the CEO of one of our state's largest companies,
is critical, yet insufficient. We can't do it with only the
30,000. But we can't do it without the 30,000 either.

You can make the organizations, companies, and institu-
tions in Kansas think of our Health ranking as a North Star
that gives us feedback on how Kansas—the state, not just
the state government—is doing. You can make it more likely

that Kansans in key roles understand the needs of the ALICE population (Asset Limited, Income Constrained, Employed—aka the working poor). You can speak to the loss needed if we are to usher in transformative change in Kansas about Health. You can bridge the factions who must work better together. You can raise the heat on existing Health efforts by asking hard, provocative questions about metrics and collaboration, as well as upstream and systemic interventions.

You can't do everything. But you can do something. And we need a lot of "somethings" to reverse our Health slide, close The Health Gap, and help Kansas lead the nation in Health.

CHAPTER 22

Ad Astra per Aspera: To the Stars, through Difficulties

I wrote this book for the movers and shakers in Kansas, the people, like you, who have outsized influence on the Health of the state, whether you realize it or not. You have tremendous authority and credibility in our state. You control budgets and other resources. You direct attention, determining whether communities, groups, or organizations take this hill or that hill. You are plugged into your community and into Kansans. Because of this, you have a tremendous opportunity to exercise leadership for Health. And Health is the single best North Star to gauge how we are doing as a state.

This book didn't provide a step-by-step comprehensive plan for exactly what should happen when and by whom. Given the diffuse power structures and systems that make up civic life, I don't believe such a plan can work. Instead, I've provided a high-level approach to transforming Kansas.

I'm suggesting that leading Health from the 30,000 and you has three parts:

1. **Mobilize** others to focus on Kansas leading the nation in Health.

2. **Disrupt** others' way of thinking by explaining Health is a leadership challenge not a Health challenge.

3. **Model** the nine mindsets needed for greater progress (described in Part Three).

When you do these things, others will care, do, and risk more to help Kansas and Kansans thrive. And as that happens, we'll be on our way toward closing The Health Gap and helping Kansas lead the nation in Health.

The title of this chapter is our state motto. I love it. To the stars through difficulties. It's a beautiful, simple, and provocative motto. It conveys a gap between where we are now and where we want to be (the stars). And it conveys that closing that gap isn't easy. Let's break down the motto piece by piece:

"To"

This is a big little word! "To" implies we are going somewhere and that we aren't satisfied with where we are now. It suggests there's someplace else we're supposed to go as Kansans. We aren't supposed to stay ranked 29th in the nation.

"The Stars"

We aren't just going anywhere. We are going to the stars, or should be at least. In those first three words our motto asks us to forever think about the gap between where we are today and excellence. "The Stars" implies a general destination, a "go West young man" type of destination that encompasses all the inspiration, optimism, and dreaming we can muster. Our motto makes clear we need a rally point. Leading the nation in Health should be that rally point.

"Through Difficulties"

This implies there are a lot of obstacles in the way. You know what helps people overcome obstacles? Leadership. Yours and mine. To reach The Stars, we'll need mindsets that help us boldly work together in the same direction.

Leading Health calls for transformation not optimization. Those good at exercising leadership optimize things. Those great at exercising leadership transform things. Kansas needs us to be great.

Optimization tinkers with the status quo.
Transformation disrupts the status quo.

Optimization keeps us within our existing box.
Transformation forces us out of the box.

Optimization feels good.
Transformation feels good, but only later.
At first it feels daunting.

Optimization makes things a bit better.
Transformation makes things exponentially better.

Closing The Health Gap takes transformation.
The 30,000 must lead that transformation. We must spur a thousand actions in the same direction. And then another thousand. And then more. With time, pressure, and focus, a new reality will be created.

From 29th to 1st – Onward Together!

Additional Notes

INTRODUCTION

This book, like my other books, is not an academic text. It's an argument that the 30,000 in Kansas need a North Star. Reversing the Health slide, as seen in the America's Health Rankings, should be that North Star. And reversing that slide, climbing the rankings, and eventually leading the nation in Health is a leadership challenge more than a health challenge.

These Additional Notes are not meant to be an academic paper bibliography or an official citing of work. But in case you want to know more about some of the topics presented in each part of this book, I have provided a few suggestions here.

PART ONE

America's Health Rankings can be found at americashealthrankings.org. Also turn to the end of this Additional Notes section to see a summary of the Kansas rankings that are referenced in this book.

Military recruiting information. The military speech referenced in this book pulls information from the US Pentagon report titled "2020 Qualified Military Available Study". A summary of that study that is easily accessible can be found at military.com in an article by Thomas Novelly from September 28, 2022.

ZIP Codes and corresponding life expectancy information is from the Robert Wood Johnson Foundation, rwjf.org. And specifically, because it is hard to find the interactive tool, in the search bar type: "Life Expectancy: Could where you live influence how long you live?"

Michael Marmot, author and former President of the World Medical Association. This book references his research from the 1970s that showed a correlation between social standing and mortality rates. Marmot's modern publications reference this original study and summarize his additional thirty years of research. See his books *The Health Gap* and *The Status Syndrome.*

United Way ALICE information can be found here: unitedforalice.org. United For ALICE Research Center Kansas has specific information for the state of Kansas: unitedforalice.org/state-overview/Kansas. The 2023 report titled *ALICE in Kansas; A Study of Financial Hardship* contains historical and current information. And the United For ALICE National Overview data has a comparison of all states: unitedforalice.org/national-overview.

Infant mortality in Kansas information can be found in at least two locations. First at the US Centers for Disease Control and Prevention website, cdc.gov. And second, at the Kansas Department of Health and Environment website, KDHE.gov. Information shared in this book was from a 2023 report covering data from 2018–2022.

Area Deprivation Index (ADI) is based on a measure created over thirty years ago by the US Health Resources & Services Administration. The University of Wisconsin Neighborhood Atlas website provides information on US neighborhoods. neighborhoodatlas.medicine.wisc.edu.

Foster care information can be found at the Kansas Department for Children and Families, dcf.ks.gov. Information in this book came from the National Youth Transition Database, Outcomes Data Snapshot: Kansas, FY 2017-2021.

Kansas population data
can be found at the United
States Census Bureau's website,
census.gov. And specifically
at census.gov/quickfacts/KS.

PART TWO

Adaptive challenges are further
discussed by Marty Linsky and
Ron Heifetz, from the Kennedy
School at Harvard, in their book
Leadership on the Line.

The Menninger Clinic
information can be found
on their website:
menningerclinic.org/centennial/
about.

PART THREE

**Race and racism differing
perspectives** are referred to in
Part Three. Here are the three
books mentioned in that section.
Ian Rowe's *Agency* reflects the
political right's perspective.
George Yancy's *Beyond Racial
Division* reflects a more centrist
perspective. Heather McGhee's
The Sum of Us reflects the
political left's perspective.

Process and structure examples
you might want to know
more about: Kansas Leadership
Center - Leadership
Transformation Grants:
kansasleadershipcenter.org/grants/
Kansas Health Foundation -
Policy Partners:
kansashealth.org/partnerships/
Network Kansas created
by the Kansas Legislature:
networkkansas.com

The William Allen White quote
is from Craig Miner's book,
*Kansas: The History of the
Sunflower State*.

Steve Feilmeier, retired CFO
of Koch Industries, KS. His
investment fund that is loaning
money to culturally competent
affordable housing developers
can be found here:
feilmeierfamilyoffice.com.

America's Health Rankings

The following is a simplified version of the Kansas summary page in the America's Health Rankings Annual Report for 2023.

The categories are the fifty-three individual measures used to come up with an overall Health score for each state.

The numbers shown here are Kansas' rank among the fifty states (1 being the state with the best outcome in that category and 50 being the state with the worst outcome in that category).

For more information visit kansashealth.org/leadinghealth or AmericasHealthRankings.org.

Measure	State Rank
Social & Economic Factors	**26**
Community and Family Safety	
Homicide	24
Occupational Fatalities	42
Public Health Funding	39
Economic Resources	
Economic Hardship Index	29
Food Insecurity	16
Income Inequality	18
Education	
Fourth Grade Reading Proficiency	34
High School Completion	18
Social Support and Engagement	
Adverse Childhood Experiences	38
High-Speed Internet	18
Residential Segregation	16
Volunteerism	7
Voter Participation	15
Physical Environment	**41**
Air and Water Quality	
Air Pollution	42
Drinking Water Violations	38
Water Fluoridation	33
Climate and Health	
Climate Policies	36
Climate Risks	28
Renewable Energy	9
Housing and Transit	
Housing With Lead Risk	36
Severe Housing Problems	8
Transportation Health Risks	4

Measure	State Rank
Clinical Care	**29**
Access to Care	
Avoided Care Due to Cost	32
Dental Care Providers	37
Mental Health Providers	37
Primary Care Providers	20
Uninsured	36
Preventive Clinical Services	
Childhood Immunizations	24
Colorectal Cancer Screening	32
Dental Visit	24
Flu Vaccination	23
HPV Vaccination	32
Quality of Care	
Dedicated Health Care Provider	19
Preventable Hospitalizations	24

Measure	State Rank
Behaviors	**31**
Nutrition and Physical Activity	
Exercise	37
Fruit and Vegetable Consumption	33
Physical Inactivity	23
Sexual Health	
Chlamydia	29
High-Risk HIV Behaviors	6
Teen Births	34
Sleep Health	
Insufficient Sleep	24
Tobacco Use	
Smoking	27

Measure	State Rank
Health Outcomes	**27**
Behavioral Health	
Drug Deaths	13
Excessive Drinking	22
Frequent Mental Distress	25
Non-medical Drug Use	25
Mortality	
Premature Death	25
Premature Death Racial Disparity	27
Physical Health	
Frequent Physical Distress	12
Low Birth Weight	13
Low Birth Weight Racial Disparity	43
Multiple Chronic Conditions	23
Obesity	34
Overall Kansas State Rank	**29**

Acknowledgements

While I get credit for being the author, I know the real authors are everyone connected to the Kansas Health Foundation. This is KHF's book. Our board of directors, staff, and many key contractors contributed significantly to the ideas expressed here.

To our board of directors—Patrick Woods, Jennifer McKenney, Junetta Everett, Don Hill, Sylvia Penner, Hyun-Jin Cho, Jill Docking, Melissa McCoy, and Alicia Thompson—thank you for encouraging me to continue my writing and for supporting this project.

Chase Willhite has been my staff partner for this project. Chase, thank you for bearing with all my "nutty ideas." You've ensured this project—which is so much more than just this book—will have the greatest possible impact in advancing our purpose: to help Kansas lead the nation in Health, eliminate the inequities that create Health disparities, and become a model for philanthropic impact. While I may have authored the book, you are authoring the broader, multi-faceted strategic communications initiative.

Todd Sattersten and Amy Buckley from Bard Press—thank you for continuing to teach me about the power of publishing and how books can change our world. Let me know when you're ready to talk about the next one!

Joy Stauber, thank you once again for providing such great creative direction for the book cover and internal page layouts.

Kenny Wilk, Tatiana Lin, and Elizabeth Ablah—thank you for being part of the early "book brain trust," which helped Todd, Chase, and me make sense of our early ideas. Your feedback throughout this process has been instrumental. Kari Bruffett, Melissa Rooker, Alan Cobb, and Joe Woodward—you each went above and beyond in reviewing the draft manuscript and offering thoughtful feedback. And to the 45 individuals who provided their feedback through the Bard Press Early Reader Program, thank you!

Joanna, Gabe, Jack, and Lizzie—thank you for your patience as I struggled to meet deadlines and when my anxiety about the project spilled over into our home life.

This book would not be possible without the lineage of great Kansans who created and guided the Kansas Health Foundation since its founding in 1985. Several have had a powerful and personal effect on me. Don Stewart—your idea to sell Wesley Medical Center and create the Foundation was bold and transformative. Marni Vliet Stone—you guided KHF with confidence and audacity, which I strive to model. Steve Coen—who we lost in 2022—taught me what it looks like to have patience and trust in partners. All three served KHF with distinction and embodied many of the mindsets described in this book.

I want to close by acknowledging several Kansans I consider mentors: Joyce Glasscock, Bill Graves, Mary Birch, Greg Musil, Bob Tomlinson (who we lost in 2025), Jon L. Stewart, David Adkins, Reggie Robinson (who we lost in 2021), Bill Snyder, and Jan Davis. You each shaped me and helped me understand the power and responsibility that comes with being part of the "30,000."

About Kansas Health Foundation

The Kansas Health Foundation (KHF) is a nonprofit organization established in 1985. We are based in Wichita, Kansas, but our mission is to improve the Health of all Kansans. As part of our strategic framework, developed by our staff and board of directors, KHF also strives to accomplish three primary purposes: empower Kansas to lead the nation in Health; eliminate the inequities that create Health disparities in Kansas; and become the model for philanthropic impact nationwide.

A Bard Press Book

Publisher: Todd Sattersten, Bard Press
Managing Editor: Amy Buckley, Bard Press
Director of Operations: Anne Ugarte, Bard Press

Jacket Designer: Joy Panos Stauber, Stauber Brand Studio
Photographer: Johan Nilsson Holmqvist, Unsplash.com
Text Designers: Joy Panos Stauber and Richard Weaver, Stauber Brand Studio
Copyeditor: Leah Brown, LeahBrownEditing
Proofreaders: Melissa Ousley and Monte Lin, Indigo: Editing, Design, and More

THE SAPLING PROGRAM
National Forest Foundation   nationalforests.org

Bard Press is committed to planting trees forward. For each tree we use
to print our books we plant two new trees through the US National Forest
Foundation's Sapling Program. These trees are planted in non-commercial,
US National Forests, and provide fresh air, clean water, and habitat protections.
To learn more go to BardPress.com/SaplingProgram.

Copyright

Leading Health: How You and 30,000 Kansans Help Communities Thrive
by Ed O'Malley

Bard Press Contact Information:
info@bardpress.com
www.bardpress.com

Ordering Information:
For additional copies, contact your favorite bookstore or email
info@bardpress.com. Quantity discounts are available.

First printing–September 2025

Publisher's Cataloging-in-Publication
(Provided by Cassidy Cataloguing Services, Inc.)

Names: O'Malley, Ed, 1975- author.
Title: Leading health : how you and 30,000 Kansans help communities thrive /
    by Ed O'Malley.
Description: Portland, Oregon : Bard Press, [2025]
Identifiers: ISBN: 9781959472209 (hardcover) | 9781959472216 (ebook)
Subjects: LCSH: Public health--Social aspects--Kansas. | Life expectancy--Social aspects--
    Kansas. | Medical care--Social aspects--Kansas. | Leadership--Kansas. | Political
    participation--Health aspects--Kansas. | Literacy--Health aspects--Kansas. |
    Broadband communication systems--Health aspects--Kansas. | BISAC: BUSINESS
    & ECONOMICS / Leadership. | MEDICAL / Public Health. | POLITICAL SCIENCE /
    Public Policy / Health Care.
Classification: LCC: RA447.K2 O53 2025 | DDC: 362.109781--dc23